LIVING & WORKING IN HONG KONG

We thought that
this might make the
good reading on the
plane out to HK !!!

We can do it !!

much love always,

Chris & Skippy

x x x

How To Books on Living & Working Abroad

Applying for a United States Visa
Backpacking Round Europe
Become an Au Pair
Do Voluntary Work Abroad
Emigrate
Finding a Job in Canada
Finding Work Overseas
Find Temporary Work Abroad
Get a Job Abroad
Get a Job in America
Get a Job in Australia
Get a Job in Europe
Get a Job in France
Get a Job in Germany
Get a Job in Hotels & Catering
Get a Job in Travel & Tourism
Live & Work in America
Live & Work in Australia
Live & Work in France
Live & Work in Germany
Live & Work in the Gulf
Live & Work in Italy
Live & Work in Japan
Live & Work in New Zealand
Live & Work in Portugal

Live & Work in Saudi Arabia
Live & Work in Spain
Living & Working in Britain
Living & Working in Canada
Living & Working in China
Living & Working in Hong Kong
Living & Working in the Netherlands
Master Languages
Obtaining Visas & Work Permits
Rent & Buy Property in France
Rent & Buy Property in Italy
Retire Abroad
Selling into Japan
Setting Up Home in Florida
Spend a Year Abroad
Study Abroad
Teach Abroad
Travel Round the World
Working Abroad
Working as a Holiday Rep
Working in Japan
Working in the Gulf
Working on Contract Worldwide
Working on Cruise Ships
Your Own Business in Europe

Other titles in preparation

The How To series now contains more than 150
titles in the following categories:

Business Basics
Family Reference
Jobs & Careers
Living & Working Abroad
Student Handbooks
Successful Writing

Please send for a free copy of the latest catalogue for full details
(see back cover for address).

LIVING & WORKING ABROAD

LIVING & WORKING IN HONG KONG

How to plan for a successful
short or long-term stay

Jeremy Gough

How To Books

Cartoons by Mike Flanagan

British Library Cataloguing in Publication Data
A catalogue record for this book is available from the British Library.

First published in 1996 by How To Books Ltd, Plymbridge House,
Estover Road, Plymouth PL6 7PZ, United Kingdom. Tel: (01752) 202301.
Fax: (01752) 202331.

Note: The material contained in this book is set out in good faith for general
guidance and no liability can be accepted for loss or expense incurred as a
result of relying in particular circumstances on statements made in the book.
The laws and regulations are complex and liable to change, and readers
should check the current position with the relevant authorities before making
personal arrangements.

Produced for How To Books by Deer Park Productions.

Typeset by Concept Communications (Design & Print) Ltd, Crayford, Kent.
Printed and bound by Cromwell Press, Broughton Gifford, Melksham, Wiltshire.

Contents

List of Illustrations

Preface

Hong Kong. Hong Kong. Just saying the name aloud is enough to send the adrenalin rushing through the veins. There is simply nowhere on earth quite like it. Whatever you want Hong Kong has it, but you have to be prepared to go out and get it. No quarter asked and no quarter given.

My wife-to-be Cindy and I first flew into Kai Tak International airport with the intention of scraping together enough money to continue our travels in south-east Asia. By the time we had got ourselves established there was simply no way we were ready to leave. Where would we go? And more importantly, why? We had found our nirvana!

This book is designed to help you get set up in Hong Kong as quickly as humanly possible. Whether that means finding work and a temporary place to stay, or a live-in maid and a school for your children, you will find what you are looking for here.

When we first touched down in the Territory, 1997 seemed a long way away and there was considerably less uncertainty about than at present. Where possible, I have tried to address the likely impact on daily life of the transfer of sovereignty. However, international politics being what it is and uncertainty being what it is, no one can say for sure what the future holds.

This book will prove an invaluable companion during the exciting early days of your new life, but ultimately, of course, you must be the author of your own Hong Kong adventure. Enjoy it.

Jeremy Gough

1
Introducing Hong Kong

It is almost impossible to mention Hong Kong without getting into a discussion about 1 July 1997, when this unique British colony is returned to Chinese sovereignty. Everybody has an opinion about what is likely to happen: 'The Chinese will ruin it.' 'It is in everybody's interests that Hong Kong continues to prosper.' 'Why would China want to interfere?'

The truth is that nobody knows for certain what the future holds. Hong Kong's situation is historically unique. There is no precedent. China has pledged to maintain it as a special administrative region with a high degree of autonomy for 50 years. It has promised that the Territory's socio-economic system and the lifestyle of its people will remain basically unchanged.

Only time will tell. One thing, however, is for sure. Hong Kong will continue to be one of the most exciting places on earth in which to live and work. Its economic resilience is legendary, the entrepreneurial spirit and work ethic of its population are unequalled, and the variety of leisure activities it offers are almost limitless.

Despite its position as one of the world's most important business centres, Hong Kong has retained much of its eastern flavour. If this is your first visit, you may be surprised by the sheer pace of life. Many visitors talk of 'sensory overload'. The colour, noise, smell and bustle of the place can quite literally be overwhelming.

To settle in quickly, it is important to try to understand just what makes Hong Kong tick.

A UNIQUE HISTORY

Before the British arrived in the 1840s Hong Kong was not seen as an inviting place to live. Its mountainous terrain offered little encouragement to farmers and its population of just a few thousand was scattered across the Territory – many of them fishermen living on boats. The future colony was also used as a base by pirates raiding the coast of China.

Hong Kong's one natural asset was its sheltered harbour strategically located on the busy trade routes of the Far East. As European trade with

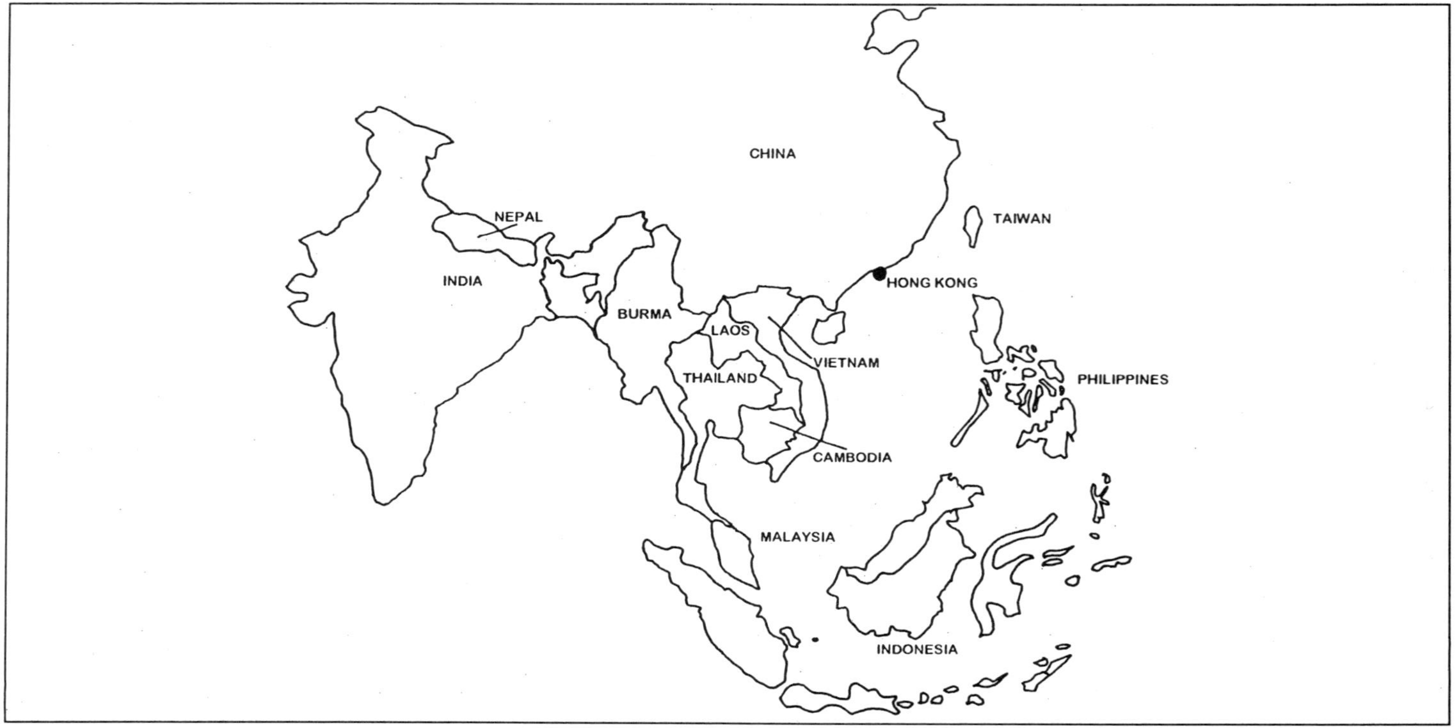

Fig. 1. Map of South-East Asia.

China increased rapidly during the early 19th century so did the merchants' need for a strategic staging post.

The Opium Wars
In an attempt to increase its export revenue, Britain was selling larger and larger amounts of opium from India to the Chinese. Peking made strident efforts to stamp out this forbidden trade. However, Britain sought to enforce its trading claims by launching naval attacks on Shanghai and Nanjing. In 1842 China ceded Hong Kong to Britain and five treaty ports were opened up to British trade. London had obtained the trading base it sought free from China's control.

Rapid development
The imperial powers' continuous struggle for trading supremacy made the Asia of the 19th century a highly unstable place. In 1898 the British, seeking greater security for Hong Kong harbour, leased the area north of Kowloon up to the Shenzhen River for 99 years. From then on, Hong Kong developed rapidly and by the early 1930s its once-tiny population had grown to almost a million. The Japanese invasion of parts of China in the late 1930s only served to speed up this process. In 1939 alone, 150,000 refugees entered Hong Kong from the mainland and by the end of that year the colony's population had reached a staggering 1.6 million.

Japanese occupation
Within days of its attack on Pearl Harbour, Japan had turned its sights on Hong Kong. Less than two weeks later, on Christmas Day 1941, the colony surrendered. It was to remain under Japanese control for three years and eight months. The end of the Second World War returned Hong Kong to British hands but did not bring peace to China. A full-scale civil war was in progress on the mainland and it brought another tidal wave of immigrants flooding into Hong Kong. Among these new arrivals were the cream of Shanghainese society. Their presence bred a degree of resentment among the Cantonese, who had always seen themselves as poor relations compared with their wealthy cosmopolitan compatriots.

Boom times
By the mid-1950s Hong Kong's population was in excess of two million and the colony's increasing prosperity only served to encourage yet more Chinese immigrants. In 1962, for example, some 140,000 refugees arrived and the British were forced to appeal to China to tighten its border controls. It was not until 1982 that Britain abandoned its touch base policy. Under this system any illegal immigrant who managed to evade border patrols and reach the urban side of the Kowloon Hills was said to have reached 'home base' and was allowed to stay.

The 1967 riots

With China's Cultural Revolution in full swing, Hong Kong was an extremely tense place in the spring of 1967. A violent industrial dispute was the catalyst for four months of serious disturbances. Left-wing activists and union organisers seized the opportunity to try to undermine colonial authority.

Demonstrations were regularly staged and poster campaigns launched calling for the end of British rule and extolling the virtues of Mao Tse-tung. Bombs were planted and rocks hurled at foreigners. There were also occasional skirmishes on the border between British and Chinese forces. It remained unclear just how much of the unrest was being orchestrated by Peking. For many, the events of 1967 confirmed the inherent instability of Hong Kong and they chose to flee the colony. However, the government of the time held its nerve and the crisis gradually defused itself.

One country, two systems

On 17 December 1984, the prime ministers of Britain and China, Margaret Thatcher and Zhao Ziyang, signed the Joint Declaration in Beijing's Great Hall of the People. Under the terms of the deal, the entire territory of Hong Kong, including Hong Kong Island itself, will be returned to Chinese sovereignty on 1 July 1997. Beijing for its part has promised to maintain the Territory's free-market economy for 50 years. It also agreed that Hong Kong's existing executive, legislative and judicial systems will remain basically in place. The people of Hong Kong, it said, will effectively be allowed to govern themselves after 1997, apart from in the areas of defence and foreign affairs.

The Tiananmen Square massacre

On 4 June 1989, soldiers of the People's Liberation Army opened fire on unarmed democracy protesters in Beijing's main square. Hundreds of civilians were to die in the days that followed. The violent suppression of the demonstration was greeted with shock and terror in Hong Kong. Confidence in the future of the colony evaporated overnight. How could China's Communist Party, which had no regard for human rights or the due process of law, be trusted to run Hong Kong fairly – whatever the Joint Declaration may or may not say?

Giant rallies were organised in Hong Kong – more than a million people took to the streets – to protest about the Communist action and a general strike was held. There was also a groundswell of support for the democracy parties in the Territory. Some voices called for Britain to renegotiate the Joint Declaration. The events in Beijing had once again put a huge question mark over the future of Hong Kong and jeopardised plans for a smooth transition of power in 1997.

Vietnamese boat people

The first group of nearly 4,000 Vietnamese refugees arrived in Hong Kong in 1975 and have provided the government with a constant headache ever since. More than 20,000 of them remain in camps across the Territory steadfastly refusing to return to their home country. Hong Kong now operates a policy of enforced repatriation but the numbers involved are not high. All new arrivals – 363 in 1994 – are screened to determine whether they are genuine refugees. Those who are deemed not to be, which is the overwhelming majority, are held in detention centres pending their repatriation.

LOOKING AT GEOGRAPHY AND CLIMATE

Situated at the south-east tip of China, the territory of Hong Kong occupies some 600 square miles of rugged terrain. It consists of the 29 square miles of Hong Kong Island itself, the Kowloon peninsula, the New Territories and a scattering of outlying islands.

Hong Kong is perfectly located for exploring the south-east Asian region. Literally next door to China, it boasts a modern international airport with a new one being built. It has direct air links with virtually every Asian country.

Typically tropical

The summers are hot and humid but over-efficient air conditioners are fitted virtually everywhere and you are more likely to need a coat inside the office than outside it. The winters are pleasantly cool for the most part although there are often several weeks in the year where it can get decidedly nippy. The best months are October, November and December when there are pleasant breezes and plenty of sunshine. May to August is the hottest time of the year and thunderstorms are frequent.

	Mean temperature (degrees C)	Mean relative % humidity	Total rainfall (mm.)
January	17.0	72	Trace
February	17.3	84	50.5
March	17.8	77	26.5
April	24.7	82	6.0
May	27.4	78	183.7
June	28.0	82	290.2
July	27.9	86	1,147.2
August	27.9	84	597.6
September	27.1	83	298.9
October	24.9	67	2.2
November	22.9	74	0.2
December	19.8	81	122.6

Fig. 2. Weather chart – 1994.

UNDERSTANDING THE PEOPLE

Hong Kong's history has been one of spectacular **population growth**. The Territory has come a long way since its days as a 'barren rock'. In recent years, although there has been a marked rise in the number of people emigrating, the population has continued to grow thanks to a combination of a high birth rate and steady immigration. At the end of 1995 Hong Kong's population stood at 6,307,900 – some 2.6 per cent or 158,800 people more than in 1994. The government estimates that by the year 2010 the population of Hong Kong could stand at a staggering 7.5 million (see Figure 3).

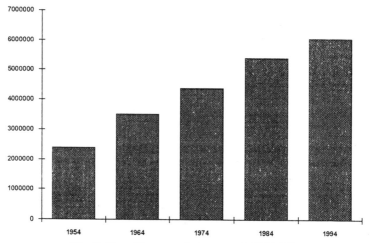

Fig. 3. Hong Kong population growth 1954-1994.

Attitudes and values

The overwhelming majority – 98 per cent – of the Hong Kong population is of Chinese origin. Of these, more than 70 per cent are **Cantonese** who originate from neighbouring Guangdong Province. The Cantonese have long been seen by China's central authorities as being slightly rebellious, although they still feel themselves to be most definitely 'Chinese'.

Great waves of **Shanghainese** fled to Hong Kong when the Communists rose to power in China. They brought with them a more cosmopolitan approach to life and a range of financial and business skills which have been of enormous help in the development of Hong Kong. Although the Shanghainese make up a relatively small percentage of the population, they are still viewed with suspicion by the Cantonese.

There are a number of non-Chinese ethnic minorities in Hong Kong. These include many long-established Indian families, thousands of Filipino maids and, of course, a large European, Australian and North American expatriate community (see Figure 4).

	Dec '91	Dec '92	Dec '93	Dec '94	Jun '95
Philippines	72,000	83,800	99,200	115,500	137,000
USA	21,000	23,500	26,100	29,900	32,100
Canada	15,000	17,500	20,400	24,700	26,900
Thailand	17,000	19,500	21,500	23,800	25,700
UK	16,000	18,400	20,300	23,700	24,800
Indonesia	–	11,000	14,700	19,700	22,800
Japan	11,000	12,300	14,000	17,600	22,100
India	18,000	18,000	18,700	19,500	20,900
Australia	13,000	14,800	16,700	18,700	20,600
Malaysia	12,000	12,600	13,000	13,800	14,400

Fig. 4. Breakdown of Hong Kong's foreign population.

Money is king

The primary motivating force of the people who live in this extraordinary colony is money. Hong Kong prides itself on the undiluted hard-edge capitalist principles on which its wealth is based. No one in Hong Kong resents the success of others. If you can find a way to make money, then good luck to you. It is taken as further proof that the Hong Kong dream really does exist. The attitude seems to be: 'If you can do it then so can I'.

This love of wealth and the trappings of wealth has promoted a strong work ethic. Everyone from the high-flying financier to the poorly-educated street hawker is prepared to work extremely long hours day in day out. The results of this industry are clear to see. On Hong Kong Island, every second person seems to be clutching a mobile phone and to quote a popular statistic, there are more Rolls Royces in Hong Kong per head of the population than anywhere else in the world.

Gambling

Hong Kong people are compulsive gamblers. Millions of dollars are invested daily in the Jockey Club's betting shop outlets. The race track at Happy Valley regularly accommodates 40,000 punters, and the one at Shatin 70,000. The Territory is affected by Mark Six lottery fever twice a week and the jackpot invariably runs into millions of dollars. The Chinese also bet regularly on Mah Jong and the sound of games in progress can be heard on most streets. The casinos of the Portuguese enclave of Macau are a short boat trip away and hundreds of Hong Kongers make the trip daily to try their luck at the roulette wheel or the poker table.

Eating

Food is an integral part of the Cantonese way of life. The people simply love to eat. The Territory's myriad dining establishments are normally packed to the rafters and the frantic clicking of chopsticks can be heard anywhere, any time. It is quite common, for example, to walk into a shop to discover the assistant busily tucking into a bowl of rice. One of the most amazing things about Hong Kong is that there are not more overweight people! Perhaps, the secret lies in the Chinese desire to balance the forces of yin (negative) and yang (positive). This philosophy is applied to all things including eating.

Shopping
After making money and eating, shopping is the next favourite pursuit of Hong Kongers. This fact is reflected in the variety and sheer volume of shopping options available in the Territory. It is more difficult to get away from shops than it is to find them. There are retail outlets specialising in everything from Chinese herbal medicines to gold and jewellery and, of course, suits. There are also numerous street stalls and hawkers adding further colour to the often chaotic street scenes. The maxim 'shop 'til you drop' is taken quite literally.

Politics
Until very recently Hong Kong people were far too busy making money to concern themselves with politics. To some extent the Tiananmen Square massacre in 1989 helped to change this, yet the turnout at recent elections was still surprisingly mediocre.

The parties of democracy are the most popular although there is strong support for pro-China groupings and for parties formed by the business lobby. The real political power remains in the hands of Governor Chris Patten and London – at least until midnight on 30 June 1997.

Attitudes to foreigners
Foreigners are very welcome in Hong Kong. Their presence signifies confidence in the future of the Territory and is a source of reassurance to the local population. However, there is a big gulf between Chinese and European culture. Friendships between Chinese and Europeans, though common, normally remain relatively formal. The Chinese are immensely proud of their culture and their identity and consider China to be the centre of the world. Western visitors are commonly referred to as 'gweilos'. This term, meaning foreign devils or white ghosts, originated as an insult but is now in wide use and is thought by many to be vaguely affectionate. Some Westerners even refer to themselves as 'gweilos'.

LANGUAGES

Cantonese and English
The predominant language in Hong Kong is **Cantonese**, a tonal dialect

which can be difficult for Westerners to master. English is also widely used, but mainly by the better-educated younger generation. English is often spoken, for example, in companies in which the senior figures are expatriates. Even in these circumstances, the Chinese naturally prefer to communicate in their native Cantonese.

The standard of English in Hong Kong is nowhere near as high as it is in Singapore. Even in tourist districts like Causeway Bay or Tsimshatsui, it is highly unlikely that newspaper sellers, taxi drivers or even many shop assistants will speak English.

Very few Westerners make the effort to become fluent in Cantonese. There are plenty of eager newcomers signing up for beginners' courses in the language but most learn little more than how to give rudimentary directions to taxi drivers. Overseas Chinese who were perhaps born and brought up in Britain find themselves in a uniquely difficult position when they come to work in Hong Kong. Their Cantonese is often patchy or non-existent and this is a source of great annoyance to the local population.

Mandarin
The imminence of the Chinese takeover has encouraged a surge of interest in **Mandarin**, the official language of the People's Republic of China. After 1997, Mandarin is mooted to become the language of business. This has prompted many firms to enrol their employees on Mandarin courses. Although written Cantonese and Mandarin are exactly the same, the spoken languages are completely different.

Tagalog
The large numbers of Filipino maids or amahs in Hong Kong can often be heard cheerfully exchanging views in their melodious native **Tagalog**. This is most evident on Sunday mornings when they gather together in parks and squares to have picnics and to trade stories about the previous week's work.

CO-EXISTING RELIGIONS

The dominant religions in Hong Kong are **Buddhism** and **Taoism**, both of which maintain a strong hold on the population, particularly the older generation. Ancestral worship is also widely practised, especially on occasions such as the Ching Ming Festival in the spring and the Cheung Yeung Festival which falls on the ninth day of the ninth moon.

Buddhism and Taoism
Despite its fame as a cosmopolitan international city, Hong Kong remains very traditional in many ways. There are some 350 temples in the Territory, about half of which are Buddhist. The majority of the others are Taoist. The

temples host fewer structured services than you might expect, with worshippers instead arriving to pray as the mood takes them.

Signs of religious observances are everywhere. You will often see offerings to the gods left in shop doorways or on the side of the road. You may notice joss sticks or pieces of fruit lying in the street. Paper offerings are also occasionally burnt on the pavement. Inside most houses, there are small shrines where offerings are made daily.

Catholic

Some five per cent of Hong Kong's population – more than 250,000 people – are Catholic. The Catholic Church has been active in the Territory since the British first arrived 1841. Most services are now conducted in Chinese although some churches do hold masses in English. There are nearly 300 Catholic schools and kindergartens catering for some 300,000 pupils.

Protestant

There are more than 50 Protestant denominations active in Hong Kong. These include Baptists, Lutherans, Adventists, Anglicans, the Church of Christ in China, Methodists and Pentecostals. The Territory's total Protestant community numbers around 300,000 people. The churches are involved in many aspects of community life and operate hundreds of kindergartens, primary schools and secondary schools as well as a number of colleges and hospitals.

Moslem

More than half of Hong Kong's 50,000 Moslems are Chinese. The rest are locally-born non-Chinese or believers from Pakistan, India, Indonesia, Malaysia, the Middle East and Africa. There are four major mosques, the largest of which can accommodate 700 worshippers.

Hindu

The are some 12,000 Hindus in Hong Kong. Their religious activities are focused on the Hindu Temple in Happy Valley on Hong Kong Island. All the important festivals such as the birth of Lord Krishna, Shivaratri, Diwali and the Holi Festival are observed.

WITNESSING AN ECONOMIC MIRACLE

One of the four 'Asian Tigers', Hong Kong is one of the world's **largest economies**. Its enormous wealth and importance are completely out of proportion to its size and population. Its standard of living is equal to, and in many cases exceeds, that of the countries of western Europe. And despite many predictions to the contrary, the imminent Chinese takeover has done little to slow the growth. Recession-proof Hong Kong continues to boom.

Live and let live

Hong Kong was once described by Professor Milton Friedman as a prime example of a 'pure *laissez faire* economy'. The Territory's incredible success is based on a fundamental belief that hard work should be rewarded and that the government should not interfere unduly in people's efforts to make their fortunes – rather let the marketplace decide. Consequently, Hong Kong remains remarkably uncluttered with red tape and regulations over matters such as starting your own business.

It would be inaccurate, however, to say there is no safety net. Since the early 1970s, great efforts have been made to reduce the unwanted side effects of unadulterated capitalism. Enormous improvements have been made in areas such as labour conditions and housing.

Made in Hong Kong

From the very beginning, Hong Kong has been known as the gateway to China. Its early growth was a direct consequence of Europe's burgeoning trading links with the Middle Kingdom. The Territory later developed a powerful reputation as a manufacturing centre. For a while, it was a standing joke that everything cheap and plastic bore the 'Made in Hong Kong' label.

Times, however, have changed. Although it may still be Hong Kong money and management behind production, nowadays most manufacturing has moved just across the border into China's special economic zones. Places like Shenzhen have become havens for Hong Kong businessmen keen to escape the Territory's high labour costs and, in some cases, the stringent safety regulations. A number of recent factory fires in China have cost hundreds of workers their lives.

The special economic zones have become bizarre ramshackle capitalist sanctuaries in the middle of Communist China. New tower blocks contrast vividly with shantytown homes, Rolls Royces drive along the potholed roads surrounded by hundreds of peasants on bicycles. The impact that Hong Kong investment is having here leaves many visitors convinced that Hong Kong is taking over China in 1997, not the other way around.

Fragrant Harbour

Hong Kong (Literally 'fragrant harbour') continues to be one of the world's busiest shipping ports. The recent construction of a number of hi-tech container terminals is designed to help it maintain the position for years to come – and to steer business away from its chief rival Singapore. The government has done all it can to ensure that export and import licenses are processed quickly and the port's efficiency has encouraged neighbouring countries, notably China, to trans-ship through Hong Kong.

Paying tax

As you might expect, Hong Kong's tax levels are low. Income tax is paid at a flat rate of 15 per cent, although a large section of the population, the relatively-low earners, do not pay tax at all. The system is designed to reward hard work and enterprise and to enable those who do well to keep most of their earnings. The government also feels that the lower the rate of tax, the more likely people are to pay it. Income tax is not taken out of salaries on a Pay As You Earn (PAYE) system. Rather, a tax bill is sent out at the end of each financial year.

Business tax rates are proportionately modest and this encourages thousands of Hong Kong's great and good to launch their own business ventures annually.

Attracting tourism

Hong Kong has not been slow to cash in on its reputation and the tourist industry is flourishing. People flock here not only to pick up cheap electronic goods and clothing but also to view some of the sensational sights on offer. A trip across the harbour, particularly at night, is an unforgettable experience, the panoramic views from the Peak are truly spectacular and everywhere the smells and sounds of Asia pervade. Many visitors are also drawn by the belief – probably mistaken – that this could be their last chance to see the 'real' Hong Kong at its booming, bustling best. The Territory is also a prime stop-over point for travellers visiting other countries in the region or seeking to take a trip into China. A range of accommodation and mind-boggling selection of restaurants and leisure pursuits are on offer.

Financial centre

Hong Kong is one of Asia's most important financial centres. The Territory has largely recovered from a series of crises in the 1980s when the reputation of the banking sector and then the stock market were severely damaged. The **Hang Seng Index** is quoted worldwide and has enjoyed a number of notable surges. However, the market is a volatile one and the Hang Seng's performance is increasingly linked to political considerations. You will find the general population has an enormous interest in the stock market. Security doormen and fishermen as well as company directors and businessmen keep a close eye on their investments.

The buck stops here

In 1983 political uncertainty sent the Hong Kong dollar into freefall on the currency markets. The then financial secretary John Brembridge reacted by pegging the local currency to the US dollar at a rate of Hong Kong $7.80 to one US dollar. The move added stability to the currency but has to some extent restricted the government's room for manoeuvre in the economic sphere. The results can be seen in Hong Kong's high rate of inflation which persistently hovers around the ten per cent mark.

CHECKLIST

● Consider the career implications of a period of work in Hong Kong.

● Weigh up the potential advantages and disadvantages for your family.

● Think about the difficulties involved in being so far away from your extended family.

● Consider what your options will be if you find Hong Kong is not for you.

CASE STUDIES

Introduction

Let us now introduce three recent arrivals in Hong Kong whose progress we will be following in the succeeding chapters. Each has come to the Territory for different reasons and with different objectives.

David Crabbe, computer consultant

David Crabbe, 40, is the new senior computer consultant in the Hong Kong office of a large international firm. He was interviewed and appointed in London and enjoys a generous expatriate package including relocation expenses, annual flights home and an accommodation allowance. David's firm will also pay for the education of his two children Oliver, 6 and Jennifer, 3. David sees the move as an incredible career opportunity, but both he and his wife Rebecca are slightly anxious about how the family will settle in such a different environment.

Tony Chettle, backpacker

University graduate Tony Chettle, 22, has been travelling in Australia and South East Asia for the past six months. He came to Hong Kong because a fellow traveller told him the Territory was good place to find work and make money. Tony's plans are fairly flexible but he would like to save up enough cash to be able to travel home through China, perhaps on board the Trans-Siberian Railway. He is hoping to find bar work to begin with. Tony is keen to make the most of his time in Hong Kong, however long or short it may prove to be.

Sarah Erikson, office worker

American Sarah Erikson, 30, gave up her job to come to Hong Kong when her boyfriend, Jack, was made redundant. They both saw it as a chance to escape their 'boring lifestyles' in Minneapolis and to try something 'really different'. Sarah is confident she will be able to find work quickly because she has a wide range of office skills and there are many international companies in Hong Kong. However, she is concerned that Jack's background as a construction worker might make him less immediately employable.

David Crabbe wants a breathing space

'These first few days have been difficult. I just hope we've made the right decision. It is so very different from anything we've experienced before. It feels strange just walking along the street. I can't believe this is our new home. I'd like to have spent a week or two settling in and having a look around the place with Rebecca and the kids but I've really been thrown in at the deep end at work. I've hardly had time to sleep let alone explore!'

Tony feels positive

'The people don't seem all that friendly here, or maybe it's just that everyone in Thailand was so nice. It seems expensive as well. I'd better get a job pretty quickly or I'm really going to be in trouble. But there's a nice buzz to the place. If I could get settled and get a bit of cash together, it might be really good.'

Sarah is overwhelmed

'I was just blown away by the place from the start. I've never been to Asia before and I guess I just wasn't prepared for it. There's so much going on, so much traffic, noise and general bustle. I had this image of Hong Kong as a super efficient modern city with big gleaming tower blocks and it is, but it is so much more as well. Everything is just so Chinese. Once you get off the main shopping roads you'd think you were in the middle of Beijing'.

DISCUSSION POINTS

1. What do you think you might like or dislike about moving to Hong Kong?

2. Go to your nearest large library and find a recent edition of one of Hong Kong's English language newspapers – *South China Morning Post, Standard, Eastern Express* – and try to get a feel for the place and what's going on there. Does it attract you or repel you?

3. If you live near a city with a Chinatown district, pay it a visit, soak up the atmosphere. Can you imagine what it would be like living there?

2
Getting Ready to Go

Before 1 July 1997, full British passport holders are granted one year's stay in Hong Kong without a visa. Citizens of other countries are given less time (three months for most Western countries, one month for Americans) but it is possible to apply for an extension when you arrive. If your visas is in need of renewal you must pay a visit to the Immigration Department (Tel: 2824 6111) complete the necessary paperwork, and attend an interview if required. It is incumbent upon you personally to ensure that your visa does not expire.

SORTING OUT THE PAPERWORK

If you do not hold a British passport, you will require a **visa** to live and work in Hong Kong prior to the transfer of sovereignty. Applications for visas are normally dealt with quickly and efficiently. If you arrive in Hong Kong as a tourist and subsequently decide you wish to stay on and work, it is possible to change your status without leaving again. You will, however, require a **letter from a potential employer** offering you a job and you may also need to show **evidence of qualifications** such as a degree certificate. This process is relatively simple and can be completed within a week. Holders of full British passports do not require visas to work in Hong Kong.

Upon arrival, visitors may be required to satisfy an immigration officer that they have **sufficient means** to support themselves during their stay. They may also be asked to produce air tickets for return or onward flights.

Meeting health requirements

Hong Kong has all but won its fight against the diseases commonly associated with tropical climates and with many of its south-east Asian neighbours. Unless you are travelling elsewhere in the region, precautions against illnesses such as malaria are largely unnecessary. However, it is important that you have kept up to date with all of the inoculations such as tetanus and diptheria which you would normally have had at home.

DECIDING HOW TO TRAVEL

Unless you are travelling to Hong Kong through China or by ferry from Taiwan or Macau, your first glimpse of the Territory will be a spectacular view of Victoria Harbour as your aircraft comes in to land at Kai Tak International Airport. Hong Kong is a popular destination and air tickets can be obtained at a very competitive price. To find the best deal, shop around as much as you can. Strangely, it is far cheaper to buy a return ticket to Hong Kong in another country than it is to buy a return ticket to the same country from Hong Kong. This is worth bearing in mind if you plan to visit your home country within the forseeable future. If you do buy a return ticket make sure you know exactly when the return portion expires.

Tidying up loose ends

Contact the post office in your home country and give them a forwarding address if you have one. Make a photocopy of your medical and dental records and those of your family. This will ease the process of registering with a new doctor and dentist in Hong Kong. Similarly, make a copy of your children's school records. Make sure that both you and your luggage are fully insured for the journey.

CHOOSING WHAT TO TAKE

Clothing

The weather in Hong Kong is temperate so you may not need as much heavy clothing as you are used to wearing. You will need a jumper and a light jacket during the winter. People here tend to dress somewhat less formally in the office than they do in most western countries. Remember that anything you forget or haven't got room to bring can probably be purchased quite cheaply in Hong Kong anyway, so don't worry too much. If you have room in your luggage a pair of sturdy walking shoes will certainly come in handy.

Furnishing your new home

When you come to rent a flat, the chances are that it is going to be unfurnished. As well as no bed and settee, that will normally also mean no cooker, no fridge and no light bulbs. Some expatriates prefer to have their own furniture shipped out – especially if their company is paying for it. Although this might help you feel at home more quickly, you should be aware that your furniture may not be suited to the Hong Kong climate. Humidity can do serious damage to upholstery and in extreme circumstances you may even find mould growing.

GOING THROUGH CUSTOMS

The normal customs restrictions apply in Hong Kong and you are prohibited from bringing goods such as narcotics and dangerous weapons into the Territory – basically all goods which are illegal anyway. There are high duties on tobacco and alcohol. The duty-free allowance is 200 cigarettes and one litre of alcohol. There are very few other restrictions on what you bring in – as long as the quantities of goods involved are not ridiculous.

Airport facilities

Kai Tak International Airport is an efficiently run modern airport with all the major facilities you would expect including restaurants, bars and banks. The Hong Kong Tourist Association (Tel: 2801 7177) has an information counter where you can pick up free visitor pamphlets. There is a **taxi rank** just outside the airport but you may find the excellent **airport bus** service cheaper and possibly even more convenient. The A1 service stops at a number of major destinations in Tsimshatsui, the A2 service stops in the Central business district and the A3 service stops in Causeway Bay. Exact change is required.

Hong Kong's new international airport at Chep Lap Kok is now scheduled to open in April 1998, about one year behind schedule. The delay was caused by political and financial wranglings between the British and Chinese governments.

COPING WITH MONEY

The **Hong Kong dollar** is the Territory's currency. Coins come in ten cents, 20 cents, 50 cents, one dollar, two dollars and five dollars. Notes in ten dollars, 20 dollars, 50 dollars, 100 dollars, 500 dollars and 1,000 dollars. There are money changers at the airport but they do charge commission of around five per cent. Foreign cash is also freely convertible in the banks where there is no commission. **Traveller's cheques** are both honoured and issued at banks throughout the Territory and a small fee is charged for changing these. If you have a credit card you may well be able to use your PIN number to obtain cash from the many automatic teller machines. Check with your credit card company to see which cash machines are available to you.

CHECKLIST

● Check that all of your health inoculations are up to date.

● Find out whether you are able to use your credit card to take out cash from automatic teller machines in Hong Kong.

- Spend a few hours phoning up some of the airline bucket shops and see how good a deal you can get on flights to the Territory.

- Make sure your passport is valid for a 'reasonable' length of time.

CASE STUDIES

David's company helps him move

'I found the actual logistics of relocating to Hong Kong to be extremely straightforward. My company handled most of the hassly things such as air tickets and temporary accommodation for when we first arrived. The only thing we really had to worry about was whether we would like the people, the job and the place . . . and I suppose what we should take with us. In the end we brought pretty much everything. It seemed silly to buy all new furniture once we arrived.'

Sarah finds the paperwork simple

'I guess I was quite surprised about how easy it was to get my working visa sorted out. I've heard that it's a nightmare for people from overseas who want to come and work in the States to get papers, but it wasn't like that at all in Hong Kong. All I had to do was to get my boss to write a letter saying that he wanted to employ me and basically why I was so suited for the job. I just took the letter and my passport to the immigration department and after a short interview they told me when I could come and pick up my visa. No problemmo.'

Tony enjoys the efficiency

'After travelling in some of the other countries of south-east Asia arriving in Hong Kong was like a breath of fresh air. The airport was clean and bright, there were efficient immigration officers and the whole place seemed so undaunting. Some of the guys at the hostel where I'm staying say that that's proof that Hong Kong is becoming more and more sanitised and characterless like Singapore. That's rubbish though. You should never knock efficiency – especially when you're arriving in a new country late at night.'

DISCUSSION POINTS

1. Do you think you should take your own furniture with you, or buy in Hong Kong?

2. Have you and your family enough suitable clothing for a humid climate?

3
Exploring the Territory

The natural beauty and variety of a territory famed for its vast skyscrapers, bustling streets and fume-filled atmosphere never ceases to amaze. Even in the heart of Hong Kong's glittering financial district you are just a short brisk walk away from deserted hill trails and staggering views across Victoria Harbour. Take an hour-long ferry trip and you will quickly be able to lose yourself in an exhausting maze of nature walks sufficiently challenging to satisfy even the most hardened of hikers.

EXPLORING HONG KONG ISLAND

Hong Kong Island occupies just 29 square miles of land which is roughly divided into a south side and a north side by a chain of rugged hills. On the north side lies the Central business district, the exclusive Peak residential area and the internationally-famous Happy Valley racetrack. On the south side, the beautiful beaches of Repulse Bay, the arts and crafts market at Stanley and the fishing harbour of Aberdeen.

Traditionally, the island is where the action is. One of the most densely-populated places on earth, some 90 per cent of its inhabitants live in tower blocks. During rush hour, an army of platform assistants is needed to shovel impatient commuters on to MTR commuter trains, crowds jostle for pole position at tram stops, and dazzling neon signs shout their Oriental message from high-rise buildings. The MTR underground system operates between Chai Wan in the east and Sheung Wan in the west. The tram line runs the length of Hong Kong Islands's northern shoreline. The island is also well served by buses and taxis. Despite the incredible density of population the island really consists of a number of small districts which, although one often runs into another, have retained quite distinctive characteristics.

Central

Central is Hong Kong's spiritual hub. This is the main business district where fortunes are made and lost. Legend has it that you can smell the money in the air as you walk down the street. You can certainly see it. Businessmen in expensive suits dash to meetings clutching mobile phones,

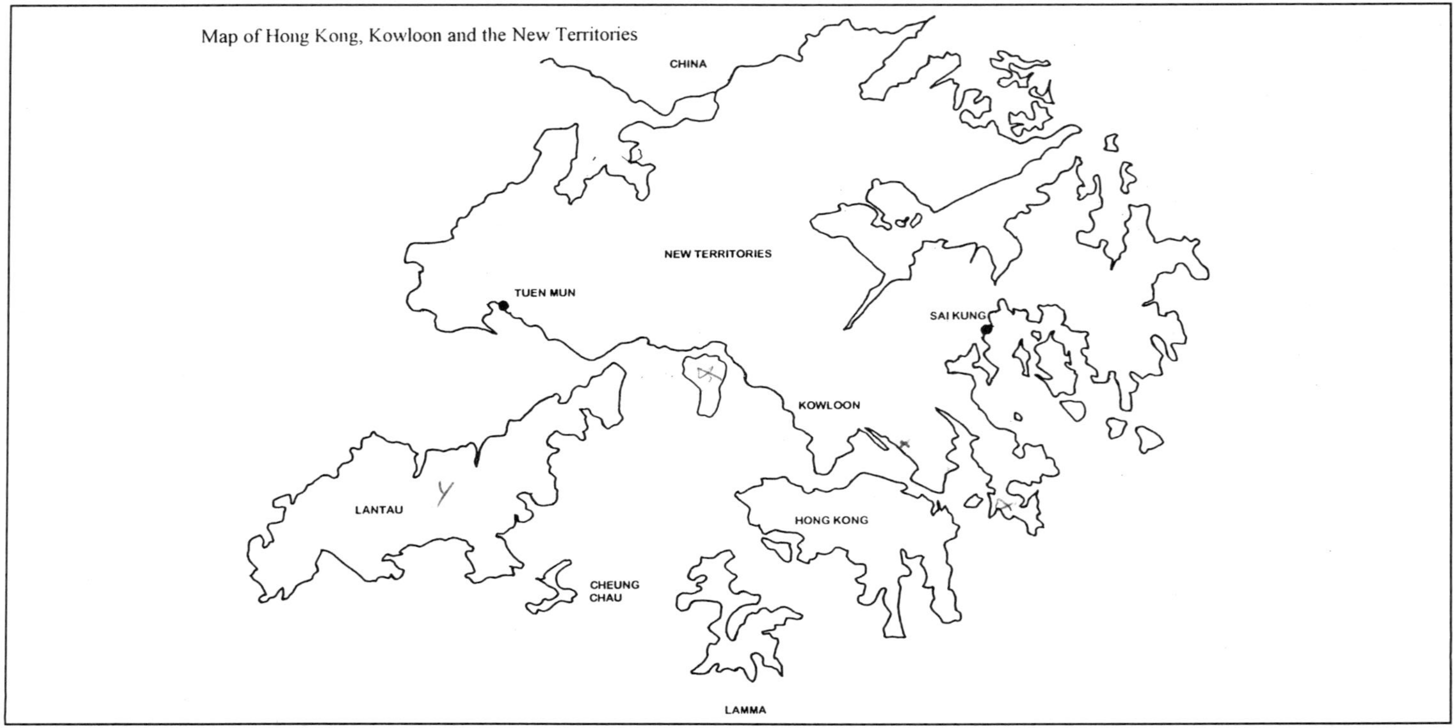

Map of Hong Kong, Kowloon and the New Territories

CHINA

NEW TERRITORIES

SAI KUNG

KOWLOON

HONG KONG

LAMMA

TUEN MUN

CHEUNG CHAU

LANTAU

Fig. 5. Map of the Territory.

young men with greedy eyes try to lure you into jewellery shops, and hard-working shoe-shine boys happily count and re-count their growing bundles of cash.

Hong Kong's major banks have their headquarters here and there are also a number of large department stores. There is also, of course, a profusion of restaurants catering mainly to the lunch-time crowd. The bar district of Lan Kwai Fong, where many people were crushed to death on New Year's Eve 1992, is still a popular haunt for the young in the evenings. The Star Ferry leaves for Kowloon every few minutes from the harbourside and many of the recreational trips on board junks commonly taken by expatriates at weekends and in the evenings also depart from here.

Causeway Bay
One of the most popular shopping districts in Hong Kong, Causeway Bay has a huge variety of stores including Marks & Spencer and some massive Japanese shopping emporiums. Many of the Territory's major hotels are also situated here. The vast Victoria Park is well used by sports enthusiasts, joggers and picnicking families and boasts attractive gardens, a model boat lake, a swimming pool and several tennis courts. The Happy Valley racetrack and government sports stadium are both a short walk away. The area is well served by tram, MTR and bus services. The harbourside offers a good view across the bay to Tsimshatsui. The Yacht Club headquarters and a profusion of house boats and small junks add to the picture postcard impression.

Wanchai
Hong Kong's 'girlie bar' district immortalised in films such as *The World of Suzy Wong* is a pale shadow of its former self. Drinking venues where young Filipino girls dance around in skimpy swimming costumes are abundant. However, the area enjoys none of the 'buzz' it boasted during the Vietnam War when American soldiers on R&R would flood in to party. There are, nonetheless, a number of decent bars and restaurants and Wanchai is still popular with tourists.

Aberdeen
Tens of thousands of people used to live in the multitude of floating homes which crammed Aberdeen harbour. Most have since moved ashore, but the area retains a unique atmosphere. Hundreds of small houseboats still bobble around the harbour and elderly ladies in sampans will quickly appear offering you a guided tour. Bargain hard.

A number of floating restaurants are also very much in evidence. The largest, the aptly-named Jumbo Restaurant, can cater for hundreds of diners at a time. The vast and impressive Ocean Park aquarium and water activities centre is not far from Aberdeen and is especially popular with children.

Stanley

The weekend market at this popular and relatively laid-back area is a major draw for overseas visitors. Selling everything from silk shirts and training shoes to carved chess sets and pencil sketches, the market is a delightful place to spend a leisurely Sunday afternoon. There are also a number of pleasant beaches and a lively strip of waterfront restaurants and bars. Many expatriates choose to make their home in Stanley.

DISCOVERING KOWLOON

Just across the harbour from Hong Kong Island lies the busy tourist district of Tsimshatsui which is packed with restaurants, shops and pubs. There is also an incredible variety of **visitor accommodation** which ranges from the misleadingly-named Chung King Mansions for budgeting backpackers to the elegant and stylish Peninsula Hotel for those who enjoy – and can afford – the finer things in life. Tsimshatsui is the place to be if you're looking for a realistic copy watch, cheap T-shirts or any manner of tourist memorabilia. The area is jam-packed with street stalls, camera shops, electronics stores and aggressive salesmen.

The enormous Harbour City complex dominates the Tsimshatsui waterfront. Situated virtually next door to the Star Ferry terminal it is easy to spend a day or more inside this air-conditioned shopper's paradise. Fine street markets proliferate near Tsimshatsui. The Temple Street market does brisk business in the evenings and offers an enjoyable mix of cheap western-style goods and products with a more authentic eastern flavour. If you are looking for an inexpensive computer or computer program then Sham Shui Po, a few stops further along the MTR line, is the place to go. The hardware is generally non-brand name, the programs generally unlicensed, but the price is invariably cheap.

But there is more to Kowloon than shops, restaurants and pubs. It won't take you long to notice the distinctive white domed roof of the Hong Kong Space Museum in Tsimshatsui. Inside, a 316-seat theatre and two astronomy exhibition halls attract hundreds of thousands of information-hungry visitors annually. Plans to develop further cultural attractions in the area are well advanced. Inside the nearby Kowloon Park the Museum of History tells the story of Hong Kong with the help of numerous exhibits. These include dioramas, street scenes and a reconstructed 100-year-old herbal medicine shop. If you eventually choose to live in the area you will find the park itself offers a welcome sanctuary from the pandemonium of every-day Hong Kong life.

Virtually all of the Territory's radio and television stations are housed on Broadcast Drive in Kowloon Tong – another area popular with expatriates. Broadcasters were encouraged to move closer together following the riots of the 1960s. The government considered these strategically important centres would be easier to protect if they were located in the same vicinity.

VENTURING INTO THE NEW TERRITORIES

Beyond the congestion of the Kowloon peninsula are the rolling hills and comparative calm of the New Territories. Stretching all the way to the Chinese border and the busy Lo Wu crossing point, the New Territories are largely unspoiled. You can still find traditional 'Chinese' farming villages which go about their business in much the same way as they have done for centuries. However, elsewhere change is taking place and many NT residents are just as interested in the fortunes of the stock market as their urban neighbours. The area around Shatin Racetrack, where races are held from September to May, has been heavily developed. There are also large towns at Tuen Mun, Tsuen Wan and Yuen Long. The fishing village of Sai Kung is a delightful place to visit and boasts several relatively clean beaches. You should beware of the sharks, however, as there have been a number of fatal attacks in recent years.

VISITING THE OUTLYING ISLANDS

You may be surprised to learn that there are 234 outlying islands in the territory of Hong Kong. Although many of these are uninhabited, several of the larger ones can be reached by regular ferry service from Hong Kong Island. The more relaxed lifestyle they offer and the far lower levels of rent they enjoy has encouraged many expatriates to make their homes there.

Lantau
By far the largest of the outlying islands, Lantau is almost twice the size of Hong Kong Island but is far less developed. Steep rugged mountains cover much of the island but you will also find some beautiful beaches and dramatic coastline. Most ferries land at Silvermine Bay (Mui Wo) and from here you can take a number of interesting trails. The determined hiker can even walk across the entire island to the historic settlement of Tai O where pedestrians are still pulled across a river in the village on a small raft. Buses are available to take you back to Silvermine Bay if the return walk doesn't appeal!

Lantau is also notable for the tallest Big Buddha monument in south-east Asia, which cost somewhere in excess of HK$60 million to construct. The statue is perched on the top of a large hill next to the Po Lin Monastery and attracts numerous visitors – especially on festival days.

The newly-developed Discovery Bay residential area is entirely different from the rest of Lantau. It is isolated geographically and culturally from
the island's other settlements but boasts all the modern amenities and a
more relaxed atmosphere than Hong Kong Island. It also enjoys a regular
high-speed service to and from Central and there is a large expatriate
community here.

Lantau's traditional lifestyle is bracing itself for a further massive
assault when the new airport at Chek Lap Kok is completed some time in
1998. The tiny island just off Lantau has basically been flattened and more
than 2,000 acres of land reclaimed from the sea in order to house the airport. A 20-mile six-lane expressway will cross over two huge suspension
bridges and through a tunnel to eventually provide a direct road and rail
link between Chek Lap Kok, Lantau, Kowloon and Hong Kong Island.

Lamma

Far smaller than Lantau, Lamma has many of its larger neighbour's advantages – pleasant beaches, spectacular hill scenery, challenging walking
trails and numerous seafood restaurants. Hungry day-trippers docking their
junks at Sok Kwu Wan and Yung Shue Wan help to create a party atmosphere in both ports' outdoor waterfront eateries. The island is traditionally
the spiritual home of western 'hippies' while they are in Hong Kong. It also
attracts many writers and artists.

Cheung Chau

From the moment you arrive at this tiny fishing island you are aware that
you are witnessing a very different side to the Hong Kong commonly por-
trayed in the media. Its narrow streets and seafaring atmosphere make it
seem somehow more authentic than even Lantau and Lamma. There are,
however, still many restaurants and bars catering to the tourist trade and the
Bun Festival every May encourages scores of people to climb a huge pile
of sugar buns in search of good fortune. The Pak Tai Temple built in 1783,
is also a big draw for visitors.

Tips for explorers

1. Get yourself a decent set of maps from the Government Publications
    Office showing Hong Kong's walking trails.

2. Find a window seat in the top deck and take a tram journey from one
    end of Hong Kong Island to the other.

3. Make sure there is plenty of film in your camera and take the Star Ferry
    from Central to Tsimshatsui.

4. Enjoy lunch at one of Sai Kung's sumptuous seafood restaurants.

5. Take an early morning ferry to one of the outlying islands.

CHECKLIST

● Decide which areas of Hong Kong you would most like to explore.

● Make the most of the Territory's spectacular scenery by taking regular country hikes.

● Do you know anyone who has access to a private or company junk?

CASE STUDIES

David enjoys the view from the Peak

'We couldn't believe it the first time we took the Peak Tram. The views are absolutely sensational from the top and we walked all the way round. We could see for miles. The kids thought it was great too, especially that frighteningly steep climb on the tram. I was so impressed I came up again after dark just to see what it was like with everything lit up. If anything it was even more spectacular.'

Tony gets away from it all

'I took the Dragon's Back trail and almost forgot where I was. It really was nice to get away from the crowds and the hassle for a few hours. I only saw about half a dozen other ramblers all the time I was up there.'

Sarah finds food fascinating

'When we took a minibus to Western there seemed to be traditional Chinese herbal shops and snake soup shops everywhere. It was fascinating watching them sell rice from giant barrels and seeing those flattened dried ducks hanging in the doorways. And what about the street hawkers selling that smelly deep-fried stuff from giant woks? Amazing.'

DISCUSSION POINTS

1. Where do you think you would most like to explore – and how would you get there?

2. If you can choose where in the Territory to live, where would it be, and why?

4
Getting Around

Hong Kong is blessed with a fantastic public transport system which is clean, efficient and punctual. In a place with such a high population density anything less would quickly result in gridlock and chaos. The government takes all reasonable steps to encourage people to get by without a car and some 90 per cent of the Territory's residents choose to do so. Every day, around ten million passenger journeys are made on public transport. Getting around in Hong Kong is not a problem.

SHOULD YOU BUY A CAR?

You may well find the prospect of living your day-to-day life without your own car a frightening one. In the west, private cars are seen almost as a birthright. The whole pattern of society seems sometimes to be moulded around the assumption that everyone owns a car. The position is exactly the opposite in Hong Kong. Take a few minutes to carefully weigh up the pros and cons.

Working out the cost

Driving in the Territory, which incidentally is done on the left hand side of the road, is expensive. Besides the actual cost of buying your car, there are a number of other charges which act as a major deterrent to would-be vehicle owners. For motor vehicles imported for use in Hong Kong a **first registration tax** is charged which is equal to some 40-60 per cent of the car's taxable value. This is generally calculated on the basis of the vehicles's published retail price. On top of this you are liable to pay an annual **vehicle licence fee** which, depending on the type of car, ranges from approximately HK$4,000 to HK$13,000. **Fuel** is also heavily taxed and is likely to be considerably more expensive than you are used to. In 1995 leaded petrol was retailing at around HK$9.24 a litre and unleaded at HK$8.80.

Parking

Parking on public streets is difficult. Meter spots are relatively rare and invariably in use. There are a number of large multi-storey car parks but there is a lot of demand for these too and finding a space can become a lottery. If you park anywhere where there is no sign actively saying that you can, you are more than likely to get a parking ticket in double quick time. Some apartment blocks offer residents' parking facilities, many more do not. Before you plunge into the car market you should obviously find out what arrangements you can make for parking near your home.

Looking at the advantages

Owning your own car does have some major advantages, particularly if you have children. On outings to the New Territories you will have the freedom to explore wherever you like. You will not have to wait for the bus or have to put up with people pushing past you in queues for the trams. You can take what you like where you like without having to worry whether you will be able to carry it. Picking up the children from school will not seem such a daunting prospect. Be warned, though, the traffic in Hong Kong, particularly on Hong Kong Island, can be a nightmare and taking the MTR can often be faster. However, if you live on the south side of Hong Kong Island or in the New Territories and work in Central you may consider a car to be an absolute necessity. In the final analysis, the decision whether to buy a car will inevitably depend on your individual circumstances, preferences and needs.

GOING UNDERGROUND – ON THE MTR

Hong Kong takes justifiable pride in its underground system, the Mass Transit Railway (MTR) (Tel: 2758 6625) which was opened in 1980. It offers a safe, speedy, reliable and comfortable mode of transport from 6am to 1am. The 24-mile long system has just three lines (see Figure 6). The first runs along the northern waterfront of Hong Kong Island from Chai Wan in the east to Sheung Wan in the west stopping at eleven other stations along the way. There are plans to extend the line further west to Kennedy Town. The second line runs under the harbour from Central on Hong Kong Island to Tseun Wan in the New Territories. It stops at 14 other stations including Tsimshatsui. The third MTR line runs from Yau Matei on Kowloon side to Quarry Bay on Hong Kong Island with eleven other stops.

Ticket prices are based on distance. Ticket machines, which do not give change, are clearly marked in all stations. They dispense plastic cards with a magnetised strip which will enable you to pass through the turnstile to the platforms. Multi-ride tickets are also available. Prices are comparable to similar systems in western capitals and the MTR offers excellent value for money. The trains operate approximately every three minutes during peak hours and every five minutes throughout the rest of the day.

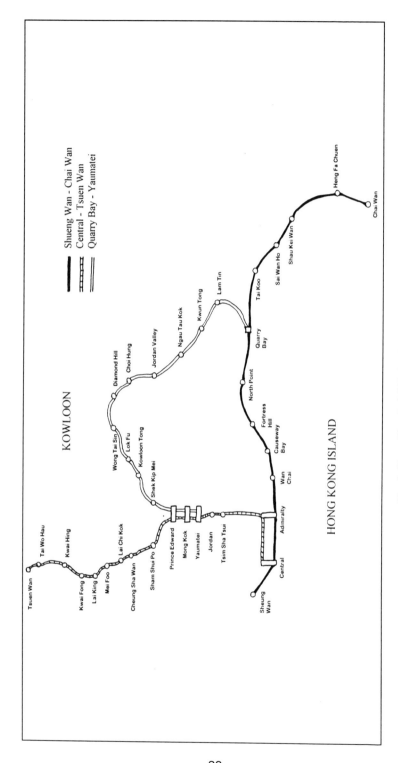

Fig. 6. Hong Kong's MTR (underground) system.

TAKING A TAXI

Taxis in Hong Kong are amazingly cheap and are consequently much in demand. Every second car on Hong Kong Island seems to be a red and silver taxi but getting one can nonetheless prove a frustrating experience. During peak periods you will quickly notice that Hong Kong does not operate on a first-come first-served basis. If a taxi stops near you, get in it – before somebody else does!

Most taxi drivers speak very little English and if your destination is not a well-known hotel or big shopping centre then try to get someone to write down the address in Chinese for you before you set off. All taxis run clearly-visible meters and although unscrupulous drivers do exist the taxi service is by and large well regulated and policed. If you are carrying luggage be prepared to pay for the privilege. Some drivers will charge you a few extra dollars, while others won't. You will also have to pay a surcharge for using the Cross-Harbour Tunnel – double the cost of actually using the tunnel. The theory being that the driver will then have to pay for himself to get back to his side of the water. In reality, of course, he will most likely find another paying customer. You will see many taxis driving around with their meters not lit or covered up. These drivers are officially off-duty but are commonly prepared to negotiate a 'special' price for a journey. Taxis in the New Territories are green and white and have a different fare structure.

CATCHING THE BUS

There is a well-used bus service in Hong Kong which criss-crosses the entire Territory. This mode of transport will be particularly useful if you do not live near an MTR station or commute to Central from places like Stanley, Repulse Bay or Kennedy Town. On Hong Kong Island, the China Motor Bus Company (Tel: 2515 1331) operates its distinctive blue and cream double-deckers on more than 80 routes. The Kowloon Motor Bus Company (Tel: 2745 4466) operates red and cream buses on some 300 routes in Kowloon and the New Territories. The New Lantau Bus Company operates eight routes on Lantau Island. Fares range from just one or two dollars to around HK$20 depending on the route and distance you are travelling. You pay as you enter the bus and drivers will require exact money.

Minibuses and maxicabs

You will see manoeuvrable 14-seater or 16-seater minibuses and maxicabs darting in and out of traffic all over Hong Kong. The minicab – pale yellow with red stripes – and maxicab – green strip with green roof – are a welcome supplement to the Territory's traditional bus service. You will find them quicker and probably slightly more expensive although prices vary depending on how far you are going. The minibuses' destination will be written on the front in large Chinese characters and then much smaller in English. It will pay you to learn some of the routes quite early on as once you understand the system it can be as convenient as getting a taxi. These vehicles will stop almost anywhere they are requested to do so. There are no bells so if you want to stop the bus you just have to shout out. The driver will normally acknowledge the request by raising a gloved hand.

If you are in a hurry be warned that drivers will sometimes stop and wait at certain spots for the bus to fill up before they move off again. If you are late for an appointment or just want to get home you will find yourself willing every passing pedestrian to hop on board so you can continue your journey.

TRAVELLING BY TRAM

Tram travel is one of the wonders of Hong Kong. It seems almost unthinkable that in such an otherwise expensive city transport can be available at such a low cost – but it is! If you have arrived in the Territory without work and are on a tight budget then this is the only way to go. The Hong Kong Tramways (Tel: 2559 8918) services run between Kennedy Town in the west of Hong Kong Island through Central to Shaukiwan in the east. Some trams will take a detour up to Happy Valley. The two-deck trams run frequently but be prepared for a battle to get on one during peak travelling times.

Progress along the 21-mile route is sometimes painfully slow, but if you are not in a rush and have a nice seat by the window the journey can be a true pleasure. The tram passes through some fascinating areas including Wanchai, Central, Western and Causeway Bay and the streets of Hong Kong are always guaranteed to supply entertainment in abundance. You pay with exact money as you leave the tram.

BOARDING THE FERRIES

The **Star Ferry** (Tel: 2522 1236) runs every few minutes between Central and Tsimshatsui. There is also a service from Central to Hunghom and from Wanchai to Tsimshatsui. The services to Tsimshatsui run from 6.30am to 11.30pm while the ferries to Hunghom run from 7am to 7.20pm. The inexpensive journey across the harbour is one of the most spectacular ferry trips you are ever likely to take and however long or short your stay in the Territory, it is a must.

Getting to outlying islands

Ferries to Hong Kong's outlying islands can be taken from the Outlying Islands Pier on Hong Kong Island. Journeys to destinations such as Lamma, Cheung Chau and Lantau normally take about one hour. The Hong Kong and Yaumatei Ferry Company (Tel: 2736 1681) operates both two- and three-deck ferries – the three-deck vessels offer a slightly more expensive - air-conditioned first-class deck.

You can get hydrofoils, ferries and catamarans to many different places in China from the China Ferry terminal in Tsimshatsui. However, if you plan to travel from here, make sure that you ask someone to write down for you the name of the port and the kind of boat you will be travelling on. Destination names in the terminal are only written in Chinese and many of the agents don't speak English.

Hydrofoils to Macau and Shenzhen make regular departures from the Hong Kong Macau Ferry terminal in Central.

CATCHING A TRAIN

The Kowloon-Canton railway (KCR) operates regular services from Hunghom railway station up into the New Territories, stopping at places such as Shatin and Tai Po. Express trains carry on through the Lo Wu border point and cross into China.

WALKING

If your journey involves a relatively short distance, why not walk? A stroll through Hong Kong's busy streets can be a very interesting experience and will give you a better understanding of local culture. Although the pavements are wide, be prepared for a few elbows as some areas get extremely busy, especially during rush hours and Saturday afternoons when everyone is out shopping.

Suggested trip

●   Take the Star Ferry from Central to Tsimshatsui, walk along Nathan Road up to Jordan MTR station and take the MTR back to Central.

CHECKLIST

●   Always carry a selection of change if you plan to use public transport.

●   Make sure you have a note of your destination in Chinese as well as English.

CASE STUDIES

Sarah takes the minibus

'I took one of the yellow-and-red minibuses from Kennedy Town to

Causeway Bay. I really appreciated the air conditioning and the comfortable seat after a hot sticky afternoon exploring the markets. The bus did stop for about ten minutes in Central waiting for passengers but I wasn't in a hurry so I didn't mind. I was a bit nervous that the driver wouldn't understand my accent when I shouted out 'stop' in Chinese, but he nodded in acknowledgement and pulled up. It was a great journey and it really made me feel like a bit of a local.'

Tony travels by tram

'I went from Wanchai to Quarry Bay by tram. I felt a bit hot and jostled at first, even though I went upstairs to avoid the main crowd. Once I got a seat it was great, especially as it is so cheap!'

David boards the hydrofoil

'I took the hydrofoil from Tsimshatsui to a business meeting in Shenzhen with two of my colleagues. The terminal itself was chaotic but once we were on the boat the journey was very pleasant. When we arrived we were approached by lots of drivers offering their services and after a bit of negotiation when the total price of the journey was agreed, we made our way towards the city centre. Traffic was horrendous and we watched cyclists carrying everything from vegetables to filing cabinets weave past as we were stuck behind a queue of lorries and limousines. By the time we arrived at the office, we hardly had any time for the meeting before we had to head back to catch our boat.'

DISCUSSION POINTS

1. Are you prepared to have to negotiate your fares on occasion?

2. Would it be a good idea to learn some Cantonese to direct taxi drivers?

3. Is there any advantage to you personally to have a car in Hong Kong?

5
Finding a Place to Live

FINDING THE AREA THAT SUITS YOU BEST

Before you start traipsing around looking at flats to rent or buy it is wise to give some thought to which area or sort of area you would like to live in:

● How close do you want to be to your work?

● Is it important that you are within strolling distance of an MTR station?

● Are you looking to get away from the madding crowds?

Fortunately, Hong Kong is a relatively small place and boasts a fantastic public transport system, so no matter where you are you will never be all that far from where you want to be. Nonetheless, convenience is of prime importance and most expatriates still choose to live on Hong Kong Island. Areas such as Happy Valley, Wanchai, Causeway Bay and Tai Koo are eternally popular because of their central locations.

Moving further out

Further afield, beyond the western-most reaches of the MTR line lies Kennedy Town which is well served by a tireless army of minibuses. Rents tend to get gradually cheaper the further away you get from the central districts and, of course, the prohibitive cost of accommodation in Hong Kong is an important consideration in choosing where to live. Mid-Levels, which can be reached from Central by a giant outdoor escalator, is another popular spot for expatriates, especially young couples. On the south side, Stanley and Repulse Bay are expatriate havens but be warned – rents are extremely high and there is no MTR service.

On Kowloon side, Tsimshatsui offers all of the major amenities and is a short MTR ride away from Hong Kong Island. Kowloon Tong has more than its fair share of overseas residents, particularly those with children as an English-speaking school is located here. Scenic spots such as Sai Kung in the New Territories have their attractions, too, particularly if you are

looking to avoid paying an outrageous proportion of your salary to the landlord. By the same token, the outlying islands offer relatively cheap accommodation if you are prepared to catch a ferry every day or if you are able
to make your living without having to do so.

RENTING OR BUYING

Renting

If you are coming to Hong Kong on a fixed-term contract or are just unsure
as to how long you are likely to stay, you will almost certainly be looking
to rent a property in the first instance. Unfortunately, rents here are among
the highest in the world. The fact that the government has now taken action
and prices are said to be heading downwards is likely to be of little comfort
to you as you write your first rent cheque. Leases are normally for a period
of a year or two years. It is possible to have a break clause inserted in a two-
year lease which will enable you to leave the property after the first twelve
months.

Checking the 'extras'
Landlords will ask for the first month's rent in advance and two months'
rent as a deposit, which is refundable at the end of your tenancy. Make sure
that you ask about rates, management fees and service charges for things
like collecting rubbish and providing a security doorman. These 'extra'
charges – ranging from around HK$500 to upwards of HK$2,000 per
month depending on your building – can obviously have a significant
impact on your budget.

Knowing the market
Make sure that you have a look at plenty of flats and in a few different areas
just to get an idea of how rent levels can vary. Be aware also that flats with
a harbour view are much sought after, by expatriates in particular, and will
be priced accordingly. As a very general rule of thumb, the higher the floor
your flat is on, the higher, too, will be the rent you will pay. Never be afraid
to negotiate on rent – the landlord is out to get as much as he possibly can
and you should be out to pay as little as you possibly can. You will soon get
to know what is and what isn't good value. Unless you are earning massive
amounts of money, enjoy a generous company housing allowance, or
choose to live on one of the outlying islands or in the New Territories, you
are unlikely to have access to your own garden. However, some residential
blocks do have communal outdoor swimming pools and barbecue areas and
these may be of particular appeal if you have a young family. In some
blocks, you may be able to make use of a roof garden.

Property for rent will be advertised in the three English language newspapers, the *South China Morning Post, Eastern Express* and the *Standard.* The *South China Morning Post* offers the most comprehensive range. You will find that some flats are advertised by private individuals but the majority by letting agencies. These will charge you the equivalent of half a month's rent for their services. There will also be a relatively modest solicitor's fee for processing your tenancy contract – this cost is normally shared between you and your new landlord.

Sharing accommodation

In the English-language newspapers you will normally find an 'Accommodation to Share' section. The prohibitive costs of living in Hong Kong make sharing a flat a practical necessity for many people – particularly the young and single. When viewing these apartments, the normal commonsense rules apply. Look not just at the standard of accommodation offered and its relative convenience to you, but also at the person with whom you will be sharing. Ask yourself the following questions:

● Are you likely to get on with him or her?

● Do you share similar interests?

● Are you likely to get the place to yourself sometimes?

● Does your potential flatmate have lots of wild friends who like to party all night?

Shared accommodation arrangements are often relatively informal. You will probably share utility bills and come to your own arrangements about dividing household chores and grocery costs. Obviously, the person who signed the initial lease agreement is the primary tenant. The amount of rent they charge you is entirely up to them and is of no concern to the real landlord.

Buying property

Hong Kong's property market is extremely volatile. Real estate speculation is rife and, until relatively recently, apartments would often change hands six or seven times before they had even been built – with each 'owner' making a tidy profit along the way. The government was eventually forced to take action to curb the spiralling property prices which were deterring overseas companies from making Hong Kong their base. In June 1995 forward selling was prohibited until six months before completion and then only based on a 100 per cent down payment. The effect was immediate and dramatic and prices fell quickly. In August 1995 a 450-square foot flat was selling for approximately HK$1.8 million – still an enormous investment.

Nobody is quite sure what impact the transfer of sovereignty will eventually have on real estate values in Hong Kong and you would be well advised to think long and hard about entering the market at such an uncertain stage.

FINDING SHORT-TERM ACCOMMODATION

There is an abundance of short-term accommodation in Hong Kong which caters specifically for the large numbers of overseas visitors. These include businessmen on two or three month contracts, backpackers who stay in the Territory just long enough to earn sufficient cash to continue their travels and newly-arrived expatriates whose companies place them in temporary accommodation until they find themselves a permanent home.

Using serviced apartments

You will find serviced apartments, which can be rented on either a weekly or a monthly basis throughout the Territory. At the lower end of the scale are single rooms which boast a bed and en-suite bathroom. A television, fridge and telephone will also be provided. Cleaners visit once a week and will change the bedding. These offer a useful starting point for new arrivals seeking a base – with a phone number and an address – from which to hunt for work. If you are looking for something more spacious – with extra bedrooms and a kitchen – these are also available. Serviced apartments are advertised regularly in the English-language press.

Staying in hotels

If you were recruited overseas you will probably spend your first few weeks in Hong Kong staying in one of the Territory's myriad hotels – probably close to your work. You will no doubt be anxious to get your family settled into a permanent home quickly, but try to be patient. Without risking the wrath of your employers, it makes sense to take this early opportunity to explore as much as possible before making a decision about which area suits you best. This will go a long way to shaping the kind of experience you and your family have during your time in Hong Kong.

Starting off in hostels

There is no shortage of low-budget hostels on Hong Kong Island itself, but Tsimshatsui is the Territory's backpacker capital. Chung King Mansions is a vast untidy looking building in the heart of Tsimshatsui which houses a rabbit warren of cheap guest houses. The overall atmosphere is drab and a touch depressing, the accommodation is generally basic, but it is in the main clean and by Hong Kong standards the staff are reasonably friendly.

If you are on a tight budget, this sort of accommodation can offer a cheap convenient short-term base, but you will no doubt want to move onward and upward as soon as you can possibly afford to.

MAKING THE MOST OF SPACE

Although you will obviously be delighted to finally move into your new home, the chances are that it is substantially more cramped than the accommodation which you are used to. It is thus more important than ever that you make the most of the space that you do have:

● put up as many wall cupboards as you can

● buy a bed with a drawer underneath

● always put things away

● hang plenty of mirrors

● keep the walls a light colour

● don't overfurnish

● use tall storage units.

CHECKLIST

● Ask advice about renting property from people you know who have been in Hong Kong for a while.

● Have a good long look through the property advertisements in the English-language media to get an idea of the market in the Territory.

● Write down a list of your anticipated expenditure for a month and decide just how much rent you really can afford to pay.

CASE STUDIES

David strikes it lucky

'The rents here are absolute shocking. I knew they were going to be high but . . . well. I just thank my lucky stars that my company is offering such a generous accommodation allowance. Rebecca and I are both absolutely delighted with the flat. It took some finding but it's just the thing. We are on the 23rd floor and have a marvellous view over Happy Valley racetrack. The children are in heaven, too, as we have a swimming pool and tennis courts as well. We are now toying with the idea of having a live-in maid.'

Tony finds the hostel expensive

'I can't see how I'm ever going to get any money together paying this sort of cash for a kip. The Chung King Mansions is all right, but it's not the kind of place you want to hang around all evening. The trouble is as soon as you go out the door you're spending again. I suppose getting a flat might work out cheaper in the long run but how am I ever going to get three months' rent together in order to afford to move in.'

Sarah starts out in a serviced apartment

'We've got one of those single room serviced apartments and it seems to be working out okay, especially as it's not forever. There's no kitchen but we've bought one of those electric slow cookers so we can make stews and things at home. And, of course, it's nice having a television so we're not tempted to go out all the time. We've been to look at a few flats and hope to be able to have enough for the deposit in about three months or so.'

DISCUSSION POINTS

1. Decide what sort of area you would like to live in.

2. Work out how much space you absolutely need to have.

3. How much extra rent are you prepared to pay to have a nice view?

4. Make sure that you have seen enough properties to know what is and what is not a good deal.

5. How long are you prepared to put up with the inconvenience of staying in short-term accommodation?

6
Looking for Work

Hong Kong's strong work ethic and resilient economy means that unemployment remains at a consistently low level – 1.9 per cent in 1994. However, the job market for expatriates is somewhat different than it is for local Chinese. If you do not speak fluent Cantonese it is unlikely you are going to get a job working in McDonald's or as an office manager. However, English language skills do offer you plenty of other employment possibilities.

GETTING A JOB BEFORE YOU GO

Hong Kong companies will often advertise for personnel overseas, most commonly in the United Kingdom. The Territory's administrative links with Britain mean UK standards have largely been adopted and British qualifications are easily understood. English is commonly spoken at the higher echelons of international firms. Keep an eye out in the national press for jobs in the Territory. You will most likely find these in the executive placement sections. People with specific skills such as surveyors, computer technicians, journalists and financial experts are likely to be in demand.

Advantages
There are several major advantages to finding a job before you go:

- you are likely to be offered a higher salary

- you may get help with your relocation expenses

- it removes a great deal of uncertainty from your first few weeks in Hong Kong.

However, don't be too downhearted if you are unable to land a job from overseas. You will find that once you arrive and are actually 'on the ground' you will be far more likely to find work. An employer will always prefer to offer a job to someone who is standing in front of his desk rather than to someone who has written a letter from several thousand miles away.

It is possible also to register with agencies which specialise in finding their clients overseas postings.

Expatriate contracts

With 1997 upon us, the days of the super-generous expatriate contract appear to be numbered, particularly in the Civil Service. But while packages are now unlikely to include such perks as a cruise back home aboard the *Canberra* at the end of a contract, there are nonetheless some very good deals to be had. Expatriate contracts will commonly include relocation expenses, annual flights home for you and your family, an accommodation allowance, an end of contract bonus, private health insurance, the cost of your children's education and a non-contributory pension scheme.

STARTING YOUR OWN BUSINESS

If you have ever harboured ambitions of starting your own business, then Hong Kong is perhaps the best place in the world in which to give it a go. There is a modest charge to register your company and to obtain a certificate of business from the Inland Revenue (Tel: 2894 5098). The Inland Revenue registration takes eight days to come through and then off you go. There are currently more than 600,000 businesses in Hong Kong with about 98 per cent of them employing fewer than 100 people. Anyone with what they think is a good business idea and the determination and confidence to give it a try is not discouraged from doing so.

Before you launch into a business venture, however, **do you homework** very carefully. Make sure you know your market, are not likely to run into major cultural or language difficulties and are working with people you can trust. There may be an awful lot of small businesses in Hong Kong but an awful lot of them don't last a year.

RESPONDING TO ADVERTISEMENTS

All three English langauge newspapers in the Territory have situations vacant columns; the most comprehensive is in the *South China Morning Post* on a Saturday. If you don't have Cantonese language skills don't waste time going for jobs where they will obviously be required. Always enclose an up-to-date CV and a covering letter in your response to advertisements. Don't be afraid to follow up your letter with a phone call. Hong Kong can be an aggressive place, particularly when it comes to employment and business. Even if you have only been in the Territory for a short time emphasise your commitment to the place and your permanence. One of the biggest fears employers have with expatriates is that they are not going to stay for very long.

USING EMPLOYMENT AGENCIES

There are numerous employment agencies in Hong Kong which can be of enormous help to you in finding work, especially if you have a particular and specific skill. The problem is that Cantonese and increasingly Mandarin are essential for many positions. Nonetheless, expatriates do often find work through these agencies and you have nothing to lose by registering.

FINDING CASUAL WORK

If you are looking for a foothold in the Territory there are casual positions coming up all the time. **Bar work** is the perennial favourite. English-style pubs in areas such as Wanchai, Tsimshatsui, Central, Stanley and Causeway Bay use a high proportion of expatriate staff. Either telephone and ask to speak to the manager or just call in on spec. If there isn't a vacancy there and then, jobs are always coming up. Be persistent and don't be afraid to exaggerate your levels of experience. If you get the job you'll just have to learn fast!

Another good casual job is **teaching English**. You will see language schools dotted all over the Territory and there is a constant demand for expatriates to come in and make conversation with students. Most schools do not require you to have English language teaching qualifications. You will see these sorts of jobs advertised in the paper. An alternative is to simply place your own advertisement offering your services on a one-to-one basis. Many expatriates are able to make quite a good living this way. The secret is to nurture several regular long-term students.

PAYING TAX

Income is taxed at a flat rate of 15 per cent, payable at the end of each tax year which runs from 1 April to 31 March. If you are used to having your income tax deducted at source each month make sure you are not caught out by the Hong Kong system of payment. Liability to salaries tax is based on the actual income of the year of assessment. During the year of assessment, a Provisional Salaries Tax charge may be made. Tax is imposed on all incomes arising in or derived from Hong Kong.

When to pay
Every April your employer will file an employer's return of remuneration

and pensions form with the Inland Revenue Department and will also provide you with a copy. The Inland Revenue will subsequently send you a salaries tax return which must be completed and filed **within one month**. You will later receive an assessment. Payment is in two instalments: the first will call for the outstanding balance of last year's tax liability and a provisional payout for next year. The remainder of the provisional tax is normally paid three months later.

Married couples

Married couples are assessed individually but may opt for joint assessment if they feel this will reduce their liability. You may claim deductions for business expenses and for charity donations. You can also claim allowances if you have unmarried children under the age of 18 or under the age of 25 if they are in full-time education.

Business tax

Businesses are liable to pay tax on any profit derived from Hong Kong. Unincorporated businesses currently pay 15 per cent profits tax and corporations 16.5 per cent.

LOOKING AFTER PENSIONS AND INVESTMENTS

If you are lucky enough to find yourself earning a salary more generous than you might have expected at home, now is a good time to consider your investment options. There is a proliferation of financial brokers and advisers in Hong Kong who will be happy to discuss the investment avenues open to you. You may wish to consider taking out an additional pension, or investing in the stock market or with an offshore institution. It is a fact that most expatriates take a wage cut when they leave the Territory so it is well worth taking advantage of any current good fortune you may be enjoying to make provisions for your future.

WORKING HOURS

Statutory office working hours in Hong Kong are similar to those of the western world. However, the work ethic here is strong and you will find that local Chinese employees will often stay in the workplace far longer than required. Many believe that this is the best way to get ahead and are keen that their bosses should see them staying late in the office. Some workers also prefer to stay in the spacious air-conditioned surroundings of the workplace rather than go back to spend the evening in sometimes over-crowded homes.

Expatriates often find themselves working far harder than they would do in their home countries. A 'work hard play hard' attitude tends to prevail among many overseas employees. Expatriates on massive packages, in some instances twice or three times what they might have been earning in the UK, often feel they have to work twice or three times as hard to justify their salaries.

Wage levels

Although the wage levels in Hong Kong are relatively high, so too is the cost of living. Salaries are determined purely by market forces and there is no legal minimum wage. Employment rights laws guarantee benefits such as statutory paid holidays and sick leave. Most employers pay a Chinese New Year Bonus, in January or February, which normally amounts to one month's wages.

Public holidays

Hong Kong's public holidays after 1997 are still the subject of negotiations between the British and Chinese governments and have yet to be announced. Traditionally, Sunday is the Territory's day off and the following 17 days are public holidays, ten of which are statutory:

- New Year's Day
- First, second and third days of the Lunar New Year
- Ching Ming Festival
- Good Friday, the next day, and Easter Monday
- Queen's birthday
- Dragon Boat Festival
- First weekday in July
- First weekday in August
- Liberation Day – last Monday in August
- Day following Chinese Mid-Autumn Festival
- Cheung Yeung Festival
- Christmas Day
- Boxing Day (first weekday after Christmas Day).

NETWORKING

Despite a population in excess of six million, Hong Kong often seems more like a village than a big city – particularly in the expatriate community. Personal contact can be vital here, especially if you are in business for yourself. The maxim 'it's not what you know, it's who you know' might well have been written about Hong Kong. Don't be afraid to put yourself about a bit. You will quickly learn where the places to be seen are in your particular line of work. Private clubs and associations are the perfect place to network. Introduce yourself to people, exchange business cards – you never know when it might pay off.

Business cards

Hong Kongers love to exchange business cards with each other. Wherever you go, whatever you are doing, you are likely to run into someone who wishes to exchange details. The actual transfer is done very formally. A new acquaintance will take his business card in both hands and will present it to you with a bow of the head. You should do the same in return.

Most cards will have a name and address in English on one side and in Chinese characters on the other. Your new Chinese name will be the Chinese word which most sounds like your English name. Many Hong Kong people have invented an English Christian name for themselves and these are often used in preference to their real names. Remember that Chinese surnames come before Christian names. For example, Mao Tse-tung's surname was Mao.

CHECKLIST

- Register your details with an employment agency which specialises in Hong Kong.

- Look in the job sections of one of the Hong Kong newspapers and try to compare wage levels with those of your home country.

- Update your CV, making sure that you emphasise your strong points when applying for certain types of job.

- If you haven't already established your own accommodation, try to obtain use of a telephone number and address to put on your job application forms.

- Practise your interview technique, focusing particularly on the reasons you are so keen to live and work in Hong Kong.

CASE STUDIES

David didn't need to make an effort

'Well, I was lucky in as much as I never really had to look for a job in Hong Kong – it just sort of happened. My company were looking for someone to come out this way to head up the operation, particularly with China now offering so many opportunities, and I just happened to be in the right place at the right time.'

Tony enjoys teaching English

'I didn't think finding a job was so much of a problem, it was getting one which paid enough for me to save that was the real challenge. I started off working at a bar in Stanley which was OK except it was a long journey from Tsimshatsui and I was spending most of my wages on transport, or at least it seemed like it. I tried a couple of other things like handing out leaflets and walking about as a sandwich board advertiser – a bit embarrassing really – but they weren't much good either. Anyway, now I'm working at a language school teaching English and I'm really enjoying it. I haven't got any qualifications or anything and it's basically just chatting to groups of five to ten students in English about anything and everything. It's quite interesting because I get to speak to some of the local people in a way that I might never get the chance to do normally. A few pupils have asked me if I'd give them private tuition so I'm hoping to gradually break out and become sort of self-employed. We'll just have to see.'

Sarah lands on her feet

'I was really in a panic for a couple of weeks. It didn't seem like there was anything for me. Anyway, one day I saw this job advertised for a personal assistant to the managing director of an international company and I just picked up the phone and called. I went in to see him that same day and he offered me the job immediately. I do a lot of travel arranging for him as well as the usual typing and dictation. I'm going to a conference in Tokyo next month which I'm really looking forward to. I'm really hopeful that this is going to be a good career move and the money's pretty good too.'

DISCUSSION POINTS

1. How would you locate the addresses of ten companies which might be able to use someone like you?

2. What points would you stress in your CV?

3. If you don't already have a job lined up, what sort of casual work might you be prepared to do in the meantime?

7
Daily Living

COPING WITH CROWDS AND HEAT

Hong Kong is one of the most crowded urban environments in the world and you may find the sheer numbers of people out on the streets difficult to deal with. The problems are often aggravated by hot clammy weather as well as the perceived rudeness of many local people. You can expect to be pushed and shoved, buffeted and knocked about, and, worst of all, those responsible won't even be aware that they've done anything to upset you. For the sake of your blood pressure and your sanity don't take any of this barging personally. You simply have to learn to adapt and survive. Tell yourself to take a deep breath and to get on with your business.

The harsh reality is that if you ever want to get on an MTR train at a busy time or if you ever want to get off a crowded tram you are going to have to learn to push and shove with the best of them. While you may find this 'me first' mentality somewhat offensive, remember that Chinese people do not find it so.

Taking time out

Try to get out into the countryside as often as you can. It can be completely reinvigorating to get away from the urban madness for a while and get your values into perspective again. Holidays can provide a welcome relief from 'crowd overload' as well. Who knows, after a couple of weeks lying on a deserted sun-drenched beach you might actually start missing all the argie-bargie and queue jumping!

For the record, the population density for the whole Territory is 5,590 per square kilometre. Kwun Tong with 52,136 people per square kilometre is one of the most densely populated districts of all.

Tip

● To see how well you cope with crowds, go to the tram stop in front of Daimaru in Causeway Bay on a Saturday afternoon.

Keeping cool

Thankfully, the Hong Kong air conditioner salesmen have done a fantastic job. Most private flats and virtually all public buildings provide a welcome relief from the unrelenting summer. Don't be afraid to dive into a shop or hotel lobby just to cool off for a few minutes. You can guarantee you won't be alone! If you are not used to such a hot humid climate, the most important thing is that you don't overdo it. You cannot expect to do as much physical work as you might have done in countries like Britain. Drink plenty of fluids to avoid dehydration. If you are taking a walk in the countryside it is absolutely essential that you take bottles of water with you.

Beware of the sun

Keep covered up. If you must wear shorts and a T-shirt then make sure you slap on plenty of suntan cream. The full threat of skin cancer is only now being recognised and fair skinned people are particularly susceptible. Try and wear a hat as much as you can – the bigger the better. The Hong Kong climate is one of the Territory's great attractions, be sensible and enjoy it.

WEATHERING TYPHOONS

Hong Kong is particularly susceptible to typhoons between June and November. These often bring with them torrential rain, high winds and flooding. Because of the Territory's rugged terrain, landslips are also a constant worry. The meteorological department tracks typhoons from the very early stages and will issue regular bulletins assessing the likely impact on Hong Kong. Because of the unpredictable nature of the storms, a typhoon warning will sometimes be issued as a precautionary measure:

- No 1 signal is hoisted when a tropical storm moves within 400 miles.

- No 3 signal indicates severe winds. Unsecured items should be moved in off the balcony.

- No 8 signal indicates a typhoon is very close. All schools are closed and most businesses shut down. You are advised to go home and tape windows.

- No 10 signal indicates a direct hit on the Territory. Hurricane force winds are expected. You should stay inside to avoid the risk of being struck by flying objects.

KEEPING SAFE AND SECURE

Despite the odd high-profile armed raid on a centrally-located jewellers, Hong Kong is a very safe place in which to live and bring up a family. The levels of street crime are relatively low and the expatriate community is to some extent insulated from the worst of the problems. Care, however, must be taken. The crowded conditions provide the perfect environment for pickpockets to ply their trade and people who are careless with their belongings or who make a show of carrying large amounts of cash or expensive items of jewellery are obvious targets.

Drugs and organised crime

The proximity of the drug-producing regions of south-east Asia has helped ensure that there are plenty of illegal substances available in Hong Kong. The Territory does have a drug problem and counselling and rehabilitation services have been established to help addicts.

The police have had some success in the ongoing fight against organised crime syndicates, but the Triad Societies still control the lucrative prostitution, extortion and drug trafficking trades in Hong Kong. There is no reason, however, to think that a law-abiding expatriate should ever find himself involved or affected by the activities of Triad gangs such as the notorious 14K, Wo Sing Woo and Sun Yeeon.

Smuggling

Cross-border smuggling remains a major problem despite the increased cooperation between the Hong Kong and Chinese authorities in the run-up to 1997. Speeding daifeis, or speedboats, regularly dash from the Territory with stolen luxury cars and other illicit goods aboard. The smugglers, who face a possible death sentence on the mainland if captured, are prepared to fire on police vessels if approached.

There is a highly-visible police presence on the streets of Hong Kong. In 1995 there were 27,000 full-time police officers and 5,700 volunteer members of the auxiliary police force. Officers are armed. Those who speak English have a red flash on their shoulder. In 1994 there were 17,232 violent crimes committed in the Territory, including 96 murders and manslaughters, 100 rapes and nearly 5,000 serious assaults. There were nearly 70,000 non-violent crimes, such as burglary, committed in the same year.

Telephone 999 to summon emergency services.

Obtaining your identity cards

In 1980 the government felt compelled to take action to curb the massive numbers of illegal immigrants flooding into Hong Kong from China. Since that date all Hong Kong residents have been required to carry a Hong Kong identity card. These must be applied for at the immigration department within 30 days of your arrival in the Territory. Be prepared to spend half a day queuing to get your card. Photographs for the card are taken at the immigration department. The immigration officer will ask to see your passport and, if it is required, will check that you have the appropriate working visa. You will also be asked to fill out a few simple forms.

New identity cards are now being issued which will be valid beyond 1 July 1997, until such time as they are replaced by identity cards issued by the government of the Hong Kong Special Administrative Region.

A policeman may ask to see your identity card at any time and you will often see people being stopped in the street by officers. It is relatively uncommon for expatriates to be stopped and checked in this random way as the measure is chiefly aimed at detecting illegal Chinese immigrants. The identity cards have also proved a useful tool in the police's fight against crime. You will find yourself using your card to do everything from hiring a video to opening a bank account.

COST OF LIVING

The imbalance between Hong Kong's huge population and its tiny geographical size means that the majority of its goods and materials have to be imported. Prices tend to rise rapidly but wages have for the most part managed to keep pace with these increases. Between 1985 and 1994 the consumer price index – which monitors items such as housing costs, fuel, food and clothing – more than doubled.

The chart in Figure 7 will give you a rough guide to the cost of living in Hong Kong.

Inflation
One of Hong Kong's perennial economic problems is that of its high rate of inflation (see Figure 8). Prices tend to go up spectacularly quickly, but happily wage levels usually keep pace.

Grocery shopping
There are a number of supermarket chains selling top-quality products at fixed prices. The biggest are Park 'N' Shop and Wellcome. Although most staple goods are stocked, you may find some of your favourite products are not. However, there are stores which cater specifically to expatriate cravings for such items such as Marmite, nachos, and tinned pumpkin. If Marks & Spencer can't help try some of the speciality shops in Pacific Place.

If you venture into the produce markets you will find prices vary on a daily basis due to the weather. About one-quarter of the vegetables sold in

Item	Retail price April 1995 HK$

Food and Drink

Bread, 'Garden Life' brand (450g)	5.50
Coffee, instant, 'Nescafe' brand (100g jar)	26.10
Tea, 'Lipton', tea-bag, 20 bags (40g)	11.60
Bacon, back, 'Tulip' brand (kg)	99.50
Hen eggs (each)	0.70
Potatoes (kg)	7.70
Beef, fresh	
Fillet (kg)	64
Best quality (kg)	48.80
Pork, fresh	
Best cut (kg)	39.90
Pork chop (kg)	47.60
Chicken, frozen, whole (kg)	16.10
Whisky, 'Red Label' brand (large bottle)	153.50
Beer, 'San Miguel' brand (large bottle)	10
Cigarettes (packet of 20)	
All brands, king size filter tip (some hotels charge higher prices)	17.50 – 25
Washing powder, 'FAB' brand (500g)	9.50

Men's clothing

Summer suit	
Imported	1,600 – 4,300
Local	700 – 2,200
Winter suit	
Imported	2,660 – 4,800
Local	930 – 2,600
Shoes	
Imported	750 – 2,490
Local	400 – 500

Women's clothing

Winter suit, locally made	460.00 – 1,200
Dress, summer, locally made	450.00 – 590
Swimming costume, locally made	150.00 – 270
Shoes, leather, locally made	180.00 – 440

Hairdressing

Women	
Shampoo and set	32.00 – 76
Full permanent wave	160.00 – 800
Men	
Haircut	52.00 – 178

Fig. 7. Sample cost of living figures.

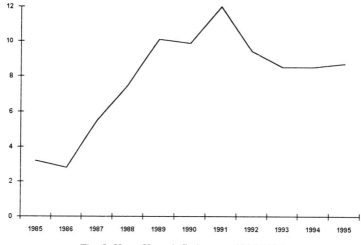

Fig. 8. Hong Kong inflation rate 1985-1995

Hong Kong are grown locally. There are normally one or two Urban Council fresh produce markets in every district. These are strictly monitored and stringent health protection measures have to be followed.

Buying furniture

There are many furniture stores in Hong Kong and, as is the Asian style, the same types of shop are often centred in one particular area. If you are searching for rattan goods, for example, you will find every second shop along a section of Queens Road East is solely dedicated to its sale. Macau is a popular place to buy furniture, particularly rosewood. The price you are offered will normally include shipment back to Hong Kong.

Second-hand furniture is another option and sometimes the previous tenant of the flat you are moving into will be seeking to sell his or her furnishings. This obviously saves a lot of headaches – even if the decor isn't always to your taste!

A final option is to buy your furniture from advertisements in the paper. The high turnover of expatriates arriving and leaving the Territory ensures a plentiful supply of second-hand items. Every week, the *Sunday Morning Post* publishes adverts from expatriates wishing to sell everything from curtain rails to chests of drawers. You may need to hire a small van or lorry for an hour or two – also advertised in the paper – so it pays to try and buy all of your large items on the same day or at least to arrange to collect them on the same day.

Banking

As a major financial centre, Hong Kong boasts numerous banks which offer their customers a fast and efficient banking service. It is a simple matter to open both savings and current accounts – all that is required is proof of identity and a nominal cash amount. You will normally be sent a cheque book and cash card within a few days. There are large numbers of cash card machines located across the Territory which enable you to withdraw cash 24 hours a day. English is widely spoken in banks.

It is quite possible for you to open up a foreign currency account, in pounds sterling or Australian dollars for example, and then to convert more cash as and when you require it. Major credit cards are accepted at the majority of retail outlets. In most cases, your salary will be paid directly into your bank account and you can make arrangements to pay your bills automatically through your bank if you wish to do so.

USING THE UTILITIES

Electricity

Hong Kong's electric current is 200 volts. If your appliances operate on a different voltage a small transformer can easily be bought to allow them to be used. Depending on the flat you live in, a whole mixture of electrical sockets may be in use. Many take round two-pin plugs but you may also find round three-pins, square two-pin and square three pins are required. The electrical supply in Hong Kong is stable and prices are reasonable.

Telephone

All local telephone calls are free on your home telephone bill and only HK$1 from the public call boxes. An international direct dialling service is available but this must be applied for. When you move into your new home you will probably need to contact Hong Kong Telecom to connect you. There will be a charge.

Telephone equipment can be bought at numerous locations throughout the Territory. Some shops specialise in selling phones disguised as anything from a banana to a model Mercedes.

Directories

As a Telecom customer you will be entitled to free telephone directories but you will have to collect these yourself from one of a number of depots. There are three residential directories covering Hong Kong, Kowloon and the New Territories as well as a business directory, a buying guide and a commercial/industrial guide.

Public phone boxes

Making a call while out on the streets is seldom a problem. There are numerous public telephone boxes and many shops and businesses will also allow you to make use of their phones free of charge. Phonecards are available and come in HK$50, HK$100 and HK$250 denominations.

Mobile phones
Mobile phones are almost *de rigeur* these days in Hong Kong. Don't expect to escape them even when you're on the bus or at the cinema!

Posting letters and packages
Letters posted in Hong Kong to a local address will arrive the following day while overseas post can take three to five days to arrive. Sending packages home can prove an expensive business and it pays to send items such as Christmas presents well in advance. The sea post service is far slower than air mail but is far cheaper. When you send packages out of Hong Kong you will be asked to fill in a customs declaration. The main post office is situated next to the Star Ferry terminal in Central. A post restante facility is available. Smaller post offices are located throughout the Territory.

Tipping
Most restaurants will add a ten per cent service charge to your bill. Nonetheless, an additional tip is usually expected. Taxi drivers will normally wait for a tip as well, but try not to overdo it. If you are travelling in a taxi with a Chinese colleague or friend you may notice that he or she will not be embarrassed to leave a far smaller tip than you might have done, if any at all. Historically, the Chinese do not usually tip. Being such a cosmopolitan city, tipping procedures in hotels and other service-related businesses are pretty much as you would find them elsewhere in the world.

ENGLISH LANGUAGE MEDIA

Newspapers and magazines
There are three English language newspapers in Hong Kong – the *South China Morning Post, Standard* and *Eastern Express*. The *South China Morning Post* is the longest established and has the most comprehensive classified sections. The *Standard* is the sister paper of one of the major Chinese dailies while the *Eastern Express*, which was only launched a few years ago, is still very much battling to establish itself. All the newspapers are very keen to guard their editorial independence as 1997 approaches and not to be influenced by direct or indirect threats from China. The *Asian Wall Street Journal* and the *International Herald Tribune* are also published here.

There are a whole host of English-language magazines written and published in Hong Kong. These include society publications, women's magazines and a number of business periodicals. You will also be able to find many special-interest publications covering subjects ranging from action sports in the region to arts and antiques. All of the major overseas English-language publications are available at newsstands or large newsagents at slightly inflated prices.

Listening to the radio

Radio Television Hong Kong (RTHK) is a government subsidised radio station offering a number of channels to English speakers. Radio Three offers light entertainment and easy listening music backed by regular news bulletins and current affairs programmes in the morning and evening. The station also relays the BBC World Service and provides a channel for classical music. Commercial Radio's 'Quote' channel has a non-speech music-only format. Metro Radio used to boast Asia's first 24-hour English language news and current affairs channel. It now operates on a bilingual format and includes light music and hourly news summaries. The British Forces Broadcasting Service provides a popular radio alternative. Its Saturday sport coverage, relaying BBC Radio Five Live, is a must for many British football fans.

Watching television

There are two English-language terrestrial TV channels – TVB Pearl and ATV World. Both are commercial stations offering a mix of imported sit-coms, films and documentaries alongside home-produced news bulletins and current affairs programmes. Most movies will carry Chinese subtitles and it is also possible to buy a Nicam television which allows the viewer to hear a dubbed Cantonese version of the film. The STAR TV satellite station now beams programmes Asia-wide but in order to receive it, your building must have the special satellite dish installed.

Video stores

Video watching is a major pastime in Hong Kong and there are scores of well-stocked video shops. The biggest chain is KPS which has all the English language films you would expect to find at home as well as sport and comedy classics. A number of foreign language movies, particularly French ones, are also available. The Chinese language section will have all the latest Hong Kong police and gangster films. All videos are subtitled.

FINDING DOMESTIC HELP

Hiring an 'amah'

The chances are that before you arrived in Hong Kong you never even dreamt of having live-in domestic help but it is something which you may soon wish to consider. Hiring an amah is surprisingly inexpensive and, if you and your partner both work, or if you have children, can help to make your stay in Hong Kong a far more positive experience. Having someone to do all the cleaning, washing, cooking and ironing will certainly give you a lot more time to do the things you want to do. The vast majority of the amahs in Hong Kong are Filipinas and most send a large proportion of their wages to family back at home. They are generally very hardworking, cheerful and loyal.

There are statutory guidelines for the employment of amahs to prevent unscrupulous families taking advantage of their good nature or of their anxiety to make a living. Contact the Hong Kong Immigration department to get details of what you as an employer will be expected to provide in terms of insurance, annual holiday, wages and living conditions. An employer is required to send his or her amah back home every two years for a holiday.

Assessing the impact
Before hiring an amah, think carefully about what sort of impact they are likely to have on your daily routine. Do you have enough space? Will you resent having another person in the house? Discuss with friends or colleagues how they have adapted to having live-in help.

The best way to find an amah is by personal recommendation but there are also regular adverts in the English language newspapers and on supermarket noticeboards. Amahs whose contracts are finished or whose previous employers are departing the Territory must find another job within a matter of weeks before they too are required to leave. Keep an eye out for advertisements from expatriate families which are keen to find a new position for their 'reliable' amah before they relocate. Filipina or Thai amahs generally have a very good standard of spoken English.

Babysitting

If you do not have an amah, finding a babysitter can be something of a problem in Hong Kong where social activities are such an important part of life. The best solution is obviously to ask a trusted acquaintance or neighbour to help you out. Unfortunately this is not always possible. There are organisations such as Rent-A-Mum (Tel: 2817 799) which provide a registered babysitting service.

CHECKLIST

● Experiment with the various newspapers, radio stations and TV channels.

● Go to the immigration department and get your identity card.

● Buy yourself a big floppy hat and plenty of suncream.

- Compare the price of goods in Hong Kong with those in your home country.

- Have a look around your local supermarkets and some of the Urban Council produce markets.

CASE STUDIES

David feels safe

'We've always been struck at how safe we feel in Hong Kong, especially as that was one of our major concerns about moving out here in the first place. Rebecca is quite happy walking about on her own, even in the evenings. Having said all of that, a couple of weeks ago she was leaving a hotel in Causeway Bay and she had her purse stolen out of her handbag. It just goes to show you can never be too careful and you should never take your safety for granted – even in Hong Kong.'

Tony wants to get fit

'I think I'm going to learn Tai Chi. It would be lovely to take something positive away from Hong Kong with me – and when you see how fit all the old people in the park are, it makes you realise that they must be doing something right.'

Sarah assesses the media

'I'm quite impressed with the newspapers out here. Considering this really isn't a majority English-speaking city there is plenty of choice and the quality is high too. The radio stations aren't bad either but I'm not too sure about the television. Maybe it's just because I'm an American and am used to so much more choice but the two terrestrial channels here really just don't cut it. They seem a bit amateurish sometimes and the way they cut into movies to switch to the commercials is unbelievable. I was watching a movie last week and they cut away from the action right in the middle of a chase scene and then came back in a few minutes later right where they'd left off. My boss at work told me he once saw them cut into a musical halfway though a song – that's really cheap.'

DISCUSSION POINTS

1. How well do you think you will cope with bustling crowds?

2. Hong Kong's high humidity can affect some expatriates quite badly. How would you try to cope?

8
Living in the East

FAMILY LIFE

The Chinese family is traditionally a tight-knit unit with a well-established hierarchy. Children are expected to show respect to their parents and to all adults. The very elderly are particularly revered and younger family members take responsibility for the care of older relatives.

Interestingly, very young children are also highly prized and are often – by western standards – quite spoiled. However, when they reach the age of four, children find their 'carefree' days are abruptly halted and they will be more frequently disciplined by their parents. The Chinese put a very high value on the birth of a boy. Women are supposedly subservient to their husbands, although this traditional view is very much under challenge in modern Hong Kong.

It is quite common for several generations of a Chinese family to live together in the same flat. To some extent the lifespan of this tradition has been prolonged by the fact that accommodation in Hong Kong is prohibitively expensive. It is only the relatively affluent who can afford to move into their own apartments.

Physical contact

Young Chinese couples tend to do less public 'canoodling' than their western counterparts. Physical contact between members of the opposite sex is not outlawed by the conventions of Hong Kong life, but it is certainly not encouraged. However, so many people have now had exposure to western ideas and culture – many youngsters having been educated overseas – that the strength of the traditional standpoint is gradually being eroded.

It is not uncommon for friends, particularly female friends, of the same sex to hold hands as they walk down the street or queue for cinema tickets. This gesture does not indicate any sexual attraction.

In general, it is best to give your Chinese friends and colleagues plenty of personal space, particularly if you do not know them all that well. Commonplace western gestures like back slapping, nudging and poking are best avoided as these may make Hong Kongers feel a little uncomfortable.

67

CELEBRATING CHINESE FESTIVALS

The following list details the five main Chinese festivals throughout the year. The precise dates are determined by the movements of the moon so the list below gives approximate times of these statutory public holidays. It is also worth bearing in mind that companies vary quite a lot when it comes to how much paid holiday they provide for Chinese New Year. Some limit leave to three days while others may close down for a couple of weeks.

- **Chinese New Year** – occurs some time between late January and February. The New Year holiday is traditionally the time to visit relatives and exchange small gifts. Children receive Lai See packets (red envelopes with money inside) and employers may distribute Lai See packets to their unmarried employees.

- **Ching Ming Festival** – occurs in early April. This holiday is to honour the dead. On the day of this festival, the cemeteries in Hong Kong are crowded with families decorating and tidying their ancestors' graves. The temples are also very busy. After paying respect to deceased relatives, many families go out for a picnic, barbecue or meal in a restaurant.

- **The Dragon Boat Festival** – occurs some time in May or June. This festival was originally held in memory of the Chinese poet Ch'u Yuen but is now widely known for its colourful dragon boat races. Competitors row to the beat of a large drum pounded out on the helm of the long narrow boats.

- **The Mid-Autumn Festival (Mooncake Festival)** – occurs in September. The festival celebrates the memory of the Han people's uprising against the Mongolians in 14th century China. The plans of the revolution were hidden inside cakes. Today, gifts of mooncakes, food and wine are exchanged and children walk around at night carrying colourful lanterns.

- **Cheung Yeung Festival** – occurs in October. This is another occasion on which Chinese people visit ancestral graves. Some people celebrate the festival by climbing hills in memory of an ancient Chinese family which fled up a mountain to escape the plague.

UNDERSTANDING SUPERSTITIONS

Chinese people in general and Hong Kong people in particular are extremely superstitious. One of the most sought-after professionals around is the **fung**

shui man. Fung shui is basically the Chinese way of maximising good luck and prosperity by aligning furniture and other objects in certain ways. Thus, offices and homes are organised to maximise good fung shui rather than to maximise efficiency or convenience. Even international companies will consult the fung shui man before building new offices as bad fung shui may keep potential customers or employees away.

Numbers, also, are of great significance in Hong Kong. The number eight sounds like prosperity in Cantonese and is therefore in great demand. Number plates bearing the digits 888 sell for a small fortune. Conversely, the figure four signifies death and is to be avoided at all costs. For example, people are extremely reluctant to live on the fourth floor of a building. The Chinese, it seems, have a superstition for just about every occasion and take the business very seriously.

SAVING FACE

The concept of 'face' is very important in Hong Kong. This makes it vital that you allow others to maintain their dignity and self-respect. To publicly carpet someone for making a mistake or to make them appear stupid or incompetent is something that should be avoided. In negotiations, or in a potentially confrontational situation, always try to leave room for compromise and to allow the person with whom you are dealing to save 'face'. With a little effort you will find it quite easy to re-phrase questions and inquiries so as not to sound as if you are apportioning blame for something but are just curious to how a matter is progressing. It is very difficult for a Chinese person to admit they have made a mistake or forgotten something so try not to put them into a position where they have to. Instead of asking: 'Haven't you found that document yet?' say something like 'Things have been really hectic lately, haven't they? Once it quietens down a bit we'll have to try and find the time to look for that document.'

THE ETIQUETTE OF A CHINESE MEAL

The Chinese love of food and eating out means that meal times are important both socially and for business. If you are invited out to share a Chinese meal, this could involve anything from noodles at the dai-pai-dong to the delicacies of a 12-course banquet. A little understanding of some of the various customs followed at the dining table will stand you in good stead.

Types of food

Cantonese
You will find more Cantonese dining establishments than any other. Fresh ingredients are always used in the preparation of Cantonese food which is

generally cooked quickly over a high heat by methods such as stir-frying and steaming. Some Cantonese specialties include abalone, shark's fin soup, steamed fish, roast pork, lots of vegetable dishes and, of course, dim sum. Many Westerners find the flavours a little too subtle and are tempted to swamp the chef's best intentions in a flood of soy sauce.

Other Chinese cuisines

Unusually, rice is not a staple in Shanghainese cuisine where Chinese buns, dumplings and noodles are the more likely accompaniments to the main course. The Shanghainese employ more oil in their cooking and tend to prefer heavier ingredients. Sichuan and Hunanese food is generally considered to be the most spicy of the Chinese cuisines with chili, pepper, onion and garlic common components. The *pièce de résistance* of Pekingese cuisine is of course the famed Peking Duck. The ceremony surrounding the serving of this dish is almost as enjoyable as the meal itself. The duck is carved in front of diners and the crispy skin is served with pancakes and a plum sauce.

Casual dining

Eating out Chinese style can be divided into two basic categories – formal and informal. If you are expected to host a meal for clients or suppliers, it may be advisable to take advice from colleagues on which kind of dining (and restaurant) would suit the occasion.

Casual-style dining in Chinese restaurants is appropriate for friends, family, colleagues and business associates who know each other well. Unless you are eating a plate of noodles from a street vendor or perhaps a takeaway from a Chinese fast-food restaurant, casual dining will involve either a family-style meal or dim sum.

Family style

One person, the host, orders the food which is placed in the middle of the table and shared. Ordering the right combination of dishes from the extensive menus is something of an art form. Your host will consider the colour, texture and taste of each dish and how it relates to the others in order to achieve a meal with just the right amount of contrast. If you are in the position of ordering the meal yourself, order one dish for each person plus one extra dish.

At the beginning of the meal, you will be given a small rice bowl, chopsticks and a spoon. The serving dishes are placed in the centre of the table, often on a turntable and – following a cue from the host that it's time to begin eating – diners help themselves. Take only small portions of each dish at a time. Many items on the menu are rather messy to eat and you will see locals taking bones from their mouths with chopsticks or simply dropping them out of their mouths onto the table. The tablecloth is expected to be messy at the finish of the meal so don't worry about spilled rice, sauce or bones.

Although mastering the use of **chopsticks** should be one of your priorities, if you are not very good with them you can ask for cutlery. Also, your Chinese companions will be happy to help out by taking your chopsticks to pick up food from the serving dishes and then filling your bowl up for you.

Tea is served with the meal in small cups or drinking glasses and you will find that your tea cup is constantly being refilled, even after only a couple of sips. Some Chinese people tap the table with their index and middle fingers while their tea is being poured as a sign of appreciation to the pourer. Beer may also be served with the meal if it is quite informal.

Dessert is a low-key event and often takes the form of fruit if it is taken at all. Also, don't expect to sit for hours over a coffee afterwards. When the food is finished, so is the meal and participants disperse fairly quickly.

Dim sum

Dim sum is another style of casual dining taken at breakfast or lunch only. Dim sum restaurants are often quite large and many are impossibly crowded on Sunday mornings. The food itself consists of many small delicacies so it is best to go with a group so you can sample a bigger variety. Diners make their choices from trolleys pushed through the restaurant. These are loaded with plates and baskets of everything from spring rolls to chicken's feet (see Figure 9). If you want something from the trolley, gesture at the 'driver' and point out your choice. They may not speak English but they are quite enthusiastic and may even suggest something they think may suit you. The plates and baskets of goodies are placed in the centre of the table and everyone helps themselves.

Tea is served with the meal and is taken from glasses or teacups. If you would like a second or third pot of tea, simply take the top off the pot and a waiter will come along and bring you more.

Formal dining

Chinese banquets are extremely formal affairs reserved for special occasions such as weddings or the honouring of a very special and important guest. Although you may well find yourself invited to a Chinese wedding during your stay in Hong Kong, your first introduction to Chinese dining, banquet-style, will probably be at your firm's annual dinner. Dress is formal. There will probably be in excess of 100 guests at the banquet and although diners sit on small tables of maybe six or eight people, the experience is very much a shared one. A small menu card may be displayed on each table so you have some idea of the dishes to follow. Teams of waiters will simultaneously serve each course, of which there may be as many as

Spring Moon
Chinese Restaurant

點心
DIM SUM MENU

灼鴿絲春卷
DEEP-FRIED SPRING ROLLS STUFFED WITH SHREDDED CHICKEN   33.00

沙律火腿卷
DEEP-FRIED SALAD ROLLS STUFFED WITH HAM   33.00

煎菜肉窩貼
PAN-FRIED DUMPLINGS STUFFED WITH MINCED PORK   33.00

香芹帶子餃
STEAMED SCALLOP DUMPLINGS WITH CELERY   33.00

炸或蒸奶黃飽
DEEP-FRIED OR STEAMED EGG YOLK BUN   33.00

叉燒酥或叉燒飽
BARBECUED PORK PUFF OR BARBECUED PORK BUN   33.00

韮菜餃
STEAMED CHINESE CHIVES DUMPLINGS   33.00

沙爹蜂巢角
DEEP-FRIED TARO STUFFED WITH MINCED PORK IN A SATAY SAUCE   33.00

鮑粒珍珠雞
STEAMED GLUTINOUS RICE WRAPPED IN A LOTUS LEAF   33.00

鮑魚鮮竹卷
STEAMED BEAN CURD SKIN ROLLS STUFFED WITH SHREDDED ABALONE   33.00

上素佛耳餃
STEAMED VEGETARIAN DUMPLINGS   .00

蝦餃
HAR GAU   36.00

魚翅干蒸燒賣
SHARK'S FIN SIU MAI   36.00

魚翅灌湯餃
SHARK'S FIN DUMPLING IN SUPREME SOUP   48.00

THE PENINSULA
HONG KONG

Fig. 9. Sample dim sum menu.

15, to each table. Rather than dishes being placed in the centre of the table to share, you are served your own individual portion. The courses themselves are usually quite small, but their sheer number ensures you will be very full by the end. Even if you are not, don't eat much of the rice or noodles as it is considered rude.

COMMUNICATING

The standard of spoken English in Hong Kong is not as high as many people expect before they arrive. You may find that even young well-educated Chinese people will have difficulty understanding you, particularly if you have a strong regional accent. You may also find that you may have difficulty understanding them at first. Be patient. Try to speak slowly and deliberately. And don't be disparaging of other people's efforts to speak English, especially as many Hong Kong people take great pride in their language ability. Try to avoid colloquialisms and jargon as much as possible.

When communication becomes really difficult, remember a smile is encouraging in any language.

Manners

You may find the Chinese attitude to politeness to be extremely confusing and contradictory. Formal greetings, the showing of respect to one's elders and superiors, and the outward maintenance of harmony are all very important to the people of Hong Kong. They simply do not respond to aggressive or disrespectful behaviour and find discord distasteful. They would rather agree with something you are saying than publicly argue with you – even though they might later go on and do something completely different from what was agreed. This bending over backwards not to create discord is then contradicted by the daily reality of aggressive people pushing past you in a bus queue or desperately trying to close the lift doors before you can get on board.

The bottom line is that the culture is different. What you may consider to be rude is completely acceptable in Hong Kong and likewise what you consider to be completely acceptable is considered to be extremely rude. Try to give and take. You are not in London or Los Angeles or Melbourne any more. A whole new code of conduct applies and it is incumbent upon you as a visitor to adapt to life in your new surroundings.

CHECKLIST

● Check if your company sponsors a team in the annual dragon boat race.

● Practise using chopsticks at home – if you can master picking up individual peanuts you know you're well on your way to proficiency.

- Find out which Chinese festival days your firm gives you time off for.

- Get together with some friends and go to a Chinese restaurant – experiment with the menu.

CASE STUDIES

David is puzzled by bad manners
'I just can't get over how rude people seem to be most of the time. Of course, you get all of the pushing and shoving and everything, but there's more to it than that. Even in the shops the staff are intolerably ill-mannered and that's when you're trying to spend some money.'

Tony enjoys the festivals
'I've really got a lot of respect for the way people here take these traditional festivals so seriously. I was out and about during the Cheung Yeung festival and you could hardly move for people off to visit their ancestors' graves. The police even had to set up crowd control measures near some cemeteries. Incredible.'

Sarah doesn't like the food
'I always thought I liked Chinese food – well I did back in the States – but it's very different here. I went out with a few of the girls from the office for lunch one day and they just ordered me some of the most disgusting things you could imagine. Yuk. Just the thought of it makes me feel sick. I just grab a burger or a pizza now.'

DISCUSSION POINTS

1. Do you like Chinese food – if not, will you cope with life in Hong Kong?

2. Are you prepared to be tolerant of unfamiliar customs and manners?

9
Health

You will find that, in general, the people of Hong Kong are a fit, healthy and energetic bunch. In fact, the overall health indices compare favourably with those in western countries. Most of the diseases commonly associated with the countries of south-east Asia such as malaria and typhoid have been all but wiped out. It is always worth remembering, however, that you are in a tropical climate and should therefore be particularly careful when cleaning fresh food in order to minimise the risk of food-borne diseases. **Tap water** is okay to drink and meets all the international standards – many people prefer to boil it anyway or buy it bottled, just to be on the safe side. The three most common causes of death in Hong Kong are cancer, heart disease and strokes.

OBTAINING HEALTH CARE

There is an excellent range of hospitals, doctors and clinics available in the Territory, providing general and specialist care to the very highest standards. Large numbers of expatriate doctors practise in Hong Kong alongside locally-trained physicians. Doctors trained at the medical schools in the Chinese University of Hong Kong and the University of Hong Kong are awarded degrees which are recognised by the General Medical Council of Great Britain. There is no National Health Service in Hong Kong offering free care such as you might find in the United Kingdom, but government medical services are available to all Hong Kong residents at a nominal charge.

Using public hospitals

There are nearly 140 government and public out-patient clinics in Hong Kong. After showing your Hong Kong identity card you will be able to get treatment at these clinics for around HK$40 – this includes medicine, the cost of laboratory tests and X-rays if required. Treatment of conditions including veneral disease and tuberculosis is completely free. There is no cost either for any maternity-related treatment. If required, a bed in a hospital ward is also available at an extremely modest rate. Emergency treatment in the case of accidents or sudden acute illness is free.

Standards of care are extremely high in public clinics but their services are very much in demand. You may find that you have a long wait to see a doctor for a non-emergency condition. Appointments are not normally given and a queuing-by-numbers system is in operation. It is advisable to arrive at the clinic in very good time as only a certain number of patients can be seen in any one day and people are often turned away and told to come back another day.

Getting to hospital

The public hospitals are well spread geographically and so wherever you choose to live you will almost certainly be within striking distance of a hospital. Villagers living in the remote parts of the New Territories are served by a flying doctor service. There are 13 public hospitals on Hong Kong Island, ten in Kowloon and 14 in the New Territories. Between them these institutions have beds for well in excess of 20,000 patients.

Using private hospitals

For all its good points, you may find that the public health care system is not for you. You, or your firm, might prefer to pay the extra cost of obtaining **private medical care**. There are twelve private hospitals in the Territory and these are widely used by the expatriate community. They have a high proportion of western doctors and nursing staff and English is widely spoken. A visit to a private practitioner will cost you in the region of HK$200 and extra charges are often made for medicines, X-rays or laboratory tests. The cost of a hospital stay can vary widely but a bed in a private room may be in the region of a HK$1,000 a day and you will also pay for all the 'extras' such as medicines and dressings.

Being prepared for the expense
Private hospitals will offer you that little bit of extra comfort and attention that you may feel you need when you are unwell. However, you must expect to pay for the privilege and unless you have adequate medical insurance, are covered by your employer's medical scheme or are extremely wealthy, you would be wise to consider the likely expense of a prolonged hospital stay. Private hospitals popular with expatriates include the Adventist (Tel: 2574 6211), Matilda (Tel: 2849 6301) and Baptist (Tel: 2339 8888).

RECEIVING DENTAL AND EYE TREATMENT

Dental care in the Territory can be expensive, particularly if you choose to go to one of the private expatriate dentists. However, patients in government hospitals are eligible to receive specialist dental treatment, and emergency care is also available at a number of district dental clinics. Free eye examinations are offered at opticians and the price of glasses and contact lenses is spectacularly reasonable in comparison with those in most western countries.

CALCULATING COSTS

Health care in Hong Kong can be incredibly cheap or frighteningly expensive. It is possible to receive an adequate standard of health care at the sometimes overworked government facilities for next to nothing. You may have to wait to be seen and the doctors and nurses may appear rushed, but you will be attended to and your condition diagnosed and treated. Private medicine offers a more comfortable level of care, but the potential costs are limitless. An extended stay in hospital is likely to make a severe dent in even the most impressive budget.

Getting insured

Many employers operate health schemes for their employees – these vary widely in the sort of treatment they cover and the costs they are prepared to meet. It is well worth finding out just what sort of medical treatment you and your family are entitled to. Private health insurance is, of course, also available and as in other parts of the world you get exactly what you pay for. If you decide to take out some extra insurance make sure you read the small print and are aware that treatment for 'pre-existing' conditions may not be covered by the policy. If you are planning to start or increase your family, you will find that policies covering pregnancy will be considerably more expensive. It will pay you to shop around to find the best deal to cover your particular needs and circumstances.

Fulfilling prescriptions

Watson's and Mannings are the two biggest western-style chemist chains in Hong Kong. The pharmacy counter will only supply prescription drugs if they have been prescribed by a doctor in Hong Kong. The stores are bright and spacious and will commonly sell a wide range of other products. Twenty-four hour pharmaceutical services are available at several of the major hospitals in the event of an emergency.

Creepy-crawlies

The tropical climate ensures the presence of some rather unwelcome house guests during the summer months – cockroaches. These unpleasant looking insects can cause considerable distress to expatriates from cooler climes. However, be reassured. The arrival of a cockroach colony does *not* mean your home is not being kept sufficiently clean! A wide variety of insect repellents and killers is available at your local supermarket to help you tackle the problem. Other 'beasties' to watch out for are poisonous centipedes whose bite can cause serious discomfort. There are a number of poisonous snakes in Hong Kong so take care, especially when out walking in the country parks.

CHECKLIST

● Find out exactly what care your medical insurance or work scheme entitles you to.

● Investigate which hospital and clinic are nearest to your home.

● Make arrangements to have your medical records transferred.

● Go and have a look around both a public and private hospital.

● Ask friends or colleagues to recommend a good dentist.

CASE STUDIES

David tests a private hospital

'Well, we didn't have long to wait to find out just how good the hospitals here were. Jennifer slipped and cracked her head just a few days after we moved into our flat. The care she received at the Adventist was absolutely first-rate, the doctor was friendly and efficient and the nurses, who were actually mainly English, were unbelievable. After a couple of days there we had a hard job persuading Jennifer to come home again.'

Tony tries the public sector

'Unbelievably, I got bitten by one of those horrible poisonous giant centipede things. It was in my shoe when I put it on one morning. It may sound funny but I can assure you it wasn't – at least at the time. I felt absolutely awful. I spent the morning traipsing around a government clinic. It took me about two-and-a-half hours before I got seen but when I did the doctor and everybody was fine. It was a bit confusing at first because I was the only Westerner there but once I had safely got hold of my number I just sat and waited my turn. I'll have no qualms about going back again if I ever need to which I hope I don't – and I'll certainly be keeping an eye out for those blooming centipedes.'

Sarah feels happy with insurance

'Well, touch wood, we haven't needed to put the medical system here to the test yet, but I've heard it's pretty good. Both Jack and I got good travel insurance before we left so we were covered in case we had any emergencies in the first few months. I've been shopping around a bit to get some more cover now we're sort of settled here. I know there is a public health care system but I guess I just feel a bit more comfortable with proper insurance. Besides, there are plenty of good deals about . . . it just comes down to peace of mind in the end.'

DISCUSSION POINTS

1. Washing fresh food and not overdoing exercise are two ways in which you can safeguard your health in a tropical, humid climate. What other precautions could you take?

2. Could you afford private health care, should you need it?

Living & Working in China

How to obtain entry and plan a successful stay

Christine Hall

China is developing rapidly. The Chinese government has opened its doors to the west, and the potential for skilled people is enormous. Whether you are planning to conduct a business in China, to teach at a school, college or university, or to go as a volunteer worker, this is the book for you. It shows you, step-by-step, how to apply for a job, how to check your employment contract, and how to obtain the visa; it gives invaluable advice on how to make friends and become part of the Chinese community: it contains survival tips, including simple cooking recipes, and a special section on how to stay healthy. Lots of checklists, contact addresses, useful words and phrases make this a comprehensive, up-to-date guide for living and working in China. Christine Hall, a specialist writer on international employment and education topics, has herself lived in China, working as a copy editor for an educational newspaper. She is a member of The Great Britain-China Centre.

£9.99, 160pp illus. 1 85703 419 8.

Available from How To Books Ltd, Plymbridge House,
Estover Road, Plymouth PL6 7PZ.
Customer Services Tel: (01752) 202301. Fax: (01752) 202331.
Please add postage & packing (£1 UK, £2 Europe, £3 world airmail).

Credit card orders may be faxed or phoned.

10
Education and Training

UNDERSTANDING THE SYSTEM

The overall excellence of the school system in Hong Kong is a reflection of the importance which the population attaches to a good education. Every morning on the MTR or on the bus, you can see parents going over that difficult piece of homework one last time with sleepy-eyed children. Some argue that education is even taken too seriously. Medical reports suggest that many Hong Kong youngsters will develop back problems in later life because of the sheer weight of books they haul to and from school each day. Even worse, there is an alarmingly high suicide rate among the Territory's students – particularly around examination time when, for some, the pressure proves just too much to bear.

School attendance for children aged 6-15 is compulsory. The government spends nearly HK$30,000 million annually on education which represents some 21 per cent of its recurrent budget and five per cent of capital expenditure. Youngsters are entitled to nine years free education up until the age of 15 – six years primary and three years secondary.

Types of schooling
Three main types of schools exist in Hong Kong:

- government schools

- aided schools which are funded by the government but run by voluntary bodies

- private schools.

Kindergartens
There are more than 800 kindergartens in Hong Kong registered under the Education Ordinance which accommodate more than 180,000 children. All kindergartens are privately run but the government often provides indirect assistance.

Primary
There are some 800 government and government-aided primary schools and 85 private establishments catering to around 500,000 pupils. For the most part, lessons are conducted in Cantonese with English being taught as a second language.

Secondary
There are three main types of secondary school in the Territory – grammar, technical and pre-vocational. They all offer a five-year course to the Hong Kong Certificate of Education (HKCEE). Places in secondary schools are allocated according to the student's ability – as determined by internal assessment – and parental choice. After attaining the HKCEE students may choose to enter a two-year sixth form course leading to the Hong Kong Advanced Level Examination for admission to tertiary institutions such as universities. Around 450,000 children attend secondary day schools – 90 per cent of them in the public sector.

Special schools
There are 63 special schools providing places for the blind, deaf, maladjusted and mentally handicapped.

English-speaking schools
The English Schools Foundation (Tel: 574 2351) was established by Government Ordinance in 1967 to provide education for English-speaking children. It currently operates a total of nine primary schools and five secondary schools. The curriculum is based on the **British state system** and the schools cater mainly for the children of expatriates. The ESF receives a per capita grant from the government based on the grants paid to other aided schools. Fees are charged to meet additional costs including the cost of hiring expatriate teachers.

Some private schools are designed for pupils whose mother tongue is English. Others cater for children who speak different European languages.

A few places may also exist for English-speaking children in the Anglo-Chinese schools which use English as the teaching medium.

FINDING THE RIGHT SCHOOL

English Schools Foundation
All of the English Schools Foundation's primary or junior schools operate a zoning system and children are normally expected to attend the school serving their residential area. If you are placed in temporary accommodation when you first arrive in the Territory your children will attend the school appropriate to that zone. On moving to a more permanent home,

your children will then normally transfer to the appropriate zone school. Admission is at all times dependent on the availability of places.

Obtaining a place

In order for your child to obtain a place in one of the English Schools Foundation's secondary schools, you or your partner must be a **resident tax-payer** in Hong Kong. There are no formal entrance examinations but children are interviewed and usually given an English language test. Demand for places is heavy and no guarantees are made about immediate admission. A zoning system also applies to secondary schools and children will normally attend the school appropriate to their place of residence. A place cannot be reserved for a child until he or she has arrived in Hong Kong and has been interviewed by the school.

All ESF schools are attended by English-speaking children of many nationalities, resulting in great diversity of race, faith and culture which gives the school an international character. Pupils of more than 50 different nationalities attend ESF schools. Around 70 per cent of the Foundation's 10,000 students come from Asian backgrounds and of that 70 per cent, ten per cent are Chinese returning to Hong Kong. Fees for the 1995-1996 academic year were HK$61,500 for secondary schools and HK$37,100 for primary schools.

Attending private schools

There are a number of private schools offering places at primary and secondary levels suitable for English-speaking children of all races. Some 100,000 pupils currently attend private schools of one description or another. Not all of these schools are run on the British pattern and for this reason are extremely popular among non-UK expatriates. For example, if you are an Australian who intends to spend two years in Hong Kong you can enrol your child in a school which follows the Australian curriculum. You may decide that this will be better for your son or daughter as it will allow him or her to make a smooth transition back into the Australian school system on returning home. Students may have to fulfill certain language and examination requirements before they are admitted to private schools.

Despite their excellent academic reputation, education at a private school in Hong Kong is, unfortunately, not cheap. Costs vary from school to school and it is best to contact schools directly to find out if places are available and what the fees are. In general, you can expect to spend around HK$50,000 annually for tuition.

Teaching methods

You will find that the huge variety of schools on offer in Hong Kong is matched by an equally broad range of teaching methods. Young expatriate teachers are commonly employed to teach the overseas curriculum in ESF and private schools. Not surprisingly, they bring to the job a western approach to education. This, of course, is eventually tempered by the experience of teaching ethnically and culturally varied classes. Teachers from the UK, Canada and Australia, for example, must quickly adapt to the challenges of dealing with youngsters from Japan, Korea and India.

The public school system reflects the Chinese belief in the value of a traditional education. When compared to teaching methods in western cultures, the Hong Kong system places more emphasis on learning facts and figures than on individual thought and expression.

GOING TO UNIVERSITY

Very few expatriates are accepted on full-time courses at Hong Kong's universities as the local demand for places outstrips availability. There are some exceptions, but mainly for those who have lived in the Territory for many years. There are currently seven government-financed institutions of higher education:

- The City University of Hong Kong

- Hong Kong Baptist University

- Lingnan College

- The Chinese University of Hong Kong

- The Hong Kong Polytechnic University

- The Hong Kong University of Science and Technology

- The University of Hong Kong.

These establishments currently provide a tertiary education to well in excess of 50,000 full- and part-time students.

ENROLLING IN ADULT EDUCATION

You will find Hong Kong offers a wide range of adult education courses, catering for all tastes and interests. The vast majority of courses are held in Cantonese. Nonetheless, there is still plenty of scope for English speakers and the normal range of adult education courses is available at various schools throughout the Territory. Most popular with new arrivals are

Cantonese courses, which are well worth taking. You might not become fluent but a few simple phrases may just be enough to make sure your taxi driver doesn't get lost!

LEARNING IN THE FUTURE

The future of Hong Kong's free and unrestricted education system was a major issue in negotiations between Britain and China over the post-1997 running of the Territory. An annex to the agreement signed by two sides guarantees this independence. Part of it reads:

> The Hong Kong Special Administrative Regions shall maintain the educational system previously practised in Hong Kong. The Hong Kong Special Administrative Region Government shall on its own decide policies in the field of culture, education, science and technology, including policies regarding the educational system and its administration, the language of instruction, the allocation of funds, the examination system, the system of academic awards and the recognition of educational and technological qualifications. Institutions of all kinds, including those run by religious and community organisations, may retain their autonomy. They may continue to recruit staff and teaching material from outside the Hong Kong Special Administrative Region. Students shall enjoy freedom of choice of education and freedom to pursue their education outside the Hong Kong Special Administrative Region.

CHECKLIST

● Write to several schools that interest you and ask for a prospectus.

● Make a point of visiting schools and talk to teachers, pupils and parents.

● Investigate which schools your child would be eligible to attend.

● If you plan to eventually return to your country of origin, find out how your child's future education may be affected by a spell in Hong Kong.

CASE STUDIES

David is happy with his son's school

'We're absolutely delighted with the way Oliver has settled in at school. The children's education was one of our major concerns about coming to Hong Kong, but now I am sure that the experience will stand them in good stead. Learning to get on with little boys and girls from all over the world can only be good for both of them. And, of course, attending a school with an English curriculum is a real plus. It's reassuring to know that there won't be any problems reintegrating if and when we do go home.'

Tony wants to learn Mandarin

'I really haven't the chance to take any courses yet – besides I'm not sure I could really afford one. I thought about enrolling for Cantonese, but I think I'd prefer to learn Mandarin. It will be of much more use when I go travelling in China.'

Sarah is learning Cantonese

'I'm getting on really well with my Cantonese. I go two evenings a week to the Island School but try to do plenty of homework as well. I've met several really nice people on the course and we all try to encourage each other. Jack thinks I'm wasting my time as we're not going to be here for ever. But it would be lovely to always have a little bit of Hong Kong in me wherever we eventually end up.'

DISCUSSION POINTS

1. Are you looking for an education which will allow your child to easily re-enter the school system of your own country?

2. Have you considered how the location of your home will affect your choice of school?

3. Are you looking for a school which will help your child to benefit from the Territory's cultural diversity?

4. Are your child's language skills likely to place any restrictions on your choice of school?

5. Does your employment package cover school fees?

11
Enjoying Your Leisure Time

Whatever you like to do in your spare time, the chances are you will have little trouble doing it in Hong Kong. The variety of leisure alternatives available is truly amazing. From tennis and scuba diving to chess and lawn bowls, the Territory has it all. There are a number of excellent private sporting clubs which boast excellent facilities but you will find the public parks, tennis courts and swimming pools are also well equipped and organised. If you prefer to spend your time eating and drinking then you will have no shortage of venues in which to do either. Eating is a favourite Hong Kong pastime and the intensity of the Territory's love affair with food is reflected in the numbers of restaurants lining its streets.

EATING OUT

It is impossible to estimate the number of eateries in Hong Kong – but there are thousands with new ones opening up every day. While Hong Kong is, of course, very much a Chinese city, the choice of restaurants reflects its international nature. It offers the perfect opportunity to sample the delights of Thai, Vietnamese, Mongolian, Filipino, Indian, Burmese, Malaysian and Japanese cuisines. Western food is also widely available. Seafood is another great favourite and a trip out to an outlying island is normally followed by a visit to one of the waterfront restaurants.

Eating out in Hong Kong is a great social occasion and is surprisingly inexpensive. You will therefore probably find yourself visiting restaurants a lot more than you are used to. *Bon appetit.*

VISITING PUBS AND CLUBS

There are numerous British style pubs in Hong Kong which are particularly popular with expatriates. The Territory's most famous bar area is Wanchai. The district's heyday as the R&R hot spot for American servicemen during the Vietnam War may be long gone but the personnel of US naval craft still flock here when their ships are in. You can still find a number of 'girlie bars' in which scantily clad females, the vast majority of them Filipino, dance seductively on a stage. If this is your thing and you would like to buy the girls a drink take plenty of money with you!

There are also several traditional pubs and nightclubs in the area. The Lan Kwai Fong district in Central consists of a couple of steep streets lined entirely with bars and clubs.

The tourist district of Tsimshatsui is also well served by pubs and clubs and you will find here a number of Australian pubs. The locally brewed beers are Carlsberg and San Miguel.

Karaoke

The Asian obsession with karaoke has taken a firm grip in Hong Kong. Karaoke rooms are hired for a set period, often an hour or two hours, and you and your party will be left alone to wail away into a microphone to your heart's content. Words and songs bounce along at the bottom of a video screen if you are a bit rusty on some of the lyrics. Karaoke can be fun. However, if you are invited along by a Chinese friend be warned that he or she may take it very seriously.

TAKING ADVANTAGE OF A SHOPPER'S PARADISE

If the people of Hong Kong are worried about the post-1997 future of the Territory, the uncertainty does not appear to have affected their seemingly limitless appetite for shopping. Despite the vast numbers of giant department stores and shopping complexes all of them remain packed late into the evening. Hong Kong's reputation as a shopper's paradise is well founded – there are not many places on earth able to match the volume and variety of goods on sale. Contrary to popular mythology, however, not all goods in Hong Kong are 'dirt cheap'. There are bargains to be had, particularly if you are seeking computer or electronic goods or inexpensive clothing, but the spiralling rents in the Territory are putting its traditional position as the world's cheapest tourist shopping centre under threat.

Shopping centres

There are 24 major shopping centres on Hong Kong Island itself. Four of them, Queensway Plaza, Admiralty Centre, United Centre and Pacific Place, are linked to each other by a covered elevated walkway. The complex situated at the Admiralty MTR station includes a giant Seibu Department store and a multi-screen cinema. The 12-storey Times Square in Causeway Bay is one of the Territory's newest shopping complexes. It also hosts a cinema and an impressive array of good restaurants. The City Plaza in Taikoo Shing which boasts a bowling alley and ice- and roller-skating rinks is particularly popular with families. Over in Kowloon, it is almost impossible to miss the vast Harbour City complex – one of the largest in the world – which includes some 600 shops.

Department stores

A number of familiar stores such as Marks & Spencer and Lane Crawford have a presence in the major shopping complexes as do some of the Japanese giants including Seibu and Matsuzakaya.

Markets

There is no shortage of pleasant street markets where you can spend an afternoon or evening seeking bargains or unusual gifts. The most famous is probably the Stanley market which is a Mecca for tourists. A variety of cheap clothes and shoes as well as Chinese paintings and carvings is available. The Temple Street evening market near Tsimshatsui is one of the Territory's most lively. Stretching for almost a mile, clothes, watches, shoes, leather goods and all manner of household items are up for sale. In Central several of the streets linking Des Voeux Road and Queen's Road are packed with stalls selling handbags, novelties and clothes. Bargains are to be had at all of these markets but be prepared to haggle.

Buying clothes

Despite the fact that Chinese people are, on average, far smaller than their western counterparts, finding clothes big enough is not really a problem. However, if you have large feet be prepared for a long slog trying to get a pair of shoes that fit.

Hong Kong is famous as a cheap place in which to buy suits. You can have suits made directly to order and the quoted price will include a number of personal fittings. Paying a visit to one of these cramped tailor shops to watch a master craftsman at work is a real education.

Consumer Council

Unfortunately, there are some unscrupulous salesmen and shopkeepers out there who seek to take advantage of the inexperienced expatriate shopper. When shopping for items such as electronic goods or jewellery it will pay you to make it quite clear that you live in the Territory and know the 'rules of the game'. Sadly, tourists are often seen as an easy mark who are unlikely to have the time or the inclination to ruin their holiday in the pursuit of shopping justice.

Shop around before you make any major purchases and always watch the sales assistant put your goods into a box. It has been known for visitors to arrive home with a completely different camera from the one they thought they had bought. Be very wary about putting a deposit down on any goods other than those which are being made to order. If you do feel you have been cheated, your best recourse is to contact the Consumer Council (Tel: 2736 3636) who will pursue a complaint on your behalf.

ENJOYING THE ARTS

It is perhaps not surprising for such a cosmopolitan society as Hong Kong that the cultural life of the Territory is so rich. There is an enormous range of artistic productions and facilities presented by the Hong Kong Government, the Regional Council, the Urban Council and various other organisations.

The best way to find out what is going on in any one week or month is to look in the local press. The *Sunday Morning Post* reviews and previews major events and lists all upcoming attractions. Shows on offer in any one week may range from a concert by a well-known international pop star to a performance by the Hong Kong Philharmonic Orchestra. Similarly, you may find an Andrew Lloyd Webber musical fresh from the West End or Broadway in town, or there may simply be a performance from an amateur drama group. Traditional Chinese entertainment including operas and plays are also on offer and the local equivalent to rock, Canto-pop, has become extremely popular and concerts are frequent. Tickets for most events are available from all Urbtix outlets. You may find the one in City Hall the easiest to locate.

Finding the venues

The possible venues for artistic entertainment are spectacularly impressive. The Hong Kong Cultural Centre (Tel: 2734 2009), which opened in Kowloon in November 1989, has become the major centre for performing arts. There is a 2,000-seat concert hall, a grand theatre seating 1,700 and a studio theatre seating up to 500 people. The City Hall (Tel: 2921 2840) also offers impressive facilities for artistic productions. It boasts a 1,500-seat concert hall, a 500-seat theatre and a 100-seat recital hall. The Hong Kong Arts Centre has three auditoriums: the 400-seat Shouson Theatre, the 200-seat Lim Por Yen Film Theatre and the 100-seat McAulay Studio.

There is also the Hong Kong Academy for Performing Arts which has two major 1,600-seat theatres and a 200-seat studio theatre.

If you are seeking something a little more alternative the Jazz Club (Tel: 2845 8477) in Central offers a variety of more intimate entertainment. The Hong Kong Coliseum (Tel: 2355 7234) can accommodate more than 12,000 people and plays host to everything from international five-a-side football competitions and basketball tournaments to rock concerts and ballet. The Queen Elizabeth Stadium (Tel: 2591 7234), frequently presents cultural entertainment.

Going to the cinema

As in other Asian countries, going out to watch a film is a very popular pastime in Hong Kong. Cinemas are normally packed and when you buy your ticket you will also have to choose a particular seat. There are a number of multi-screen cinemas in the Territory commonly located in the big shopping complexes. All of the major Hollywood release films come here and these are supplemented by an endless stream of often extremely violent Hong Kong made films. Jackie Chan is the biggest box office attraction in the Territory outstripping even the likes of Arnold Schwarzenegger and Sylvester Stallone.

All English films will carry Chinese sub-titles and all Chinese films will carry English sub-titles, although in the latter case the standard of the translation may make it extremely difficult for you to follow the plot. English, French and German films may be watched at venues run by The British Council, Alliance Française and Goethe Institute respectively.

Attending special events

Special festivals and events take place in Hong Kong all of the time. The Hong Kong Arts Festival comprises four weeks of music and drama from around the world between January and February. The Fringe Festival takes place at the same time and provides daily entertainment on the streets as well as at the Fringe Club in Central. The popular Hong Kong International Film Festival runs for two weeks every April and shows movies from virtually every country in the world. The biennial festival of Asian Arts which takes place in October and November in even-numbered years attracts more than 150 artistic performances from across the region.

Using public libraries

Most public libraries have a reasonable selection of English language books. Contact the Urban Council to find the one most convenient for you. Most libraries are now computerised to enable you to speedily track down a particular book. The central library is at City Hall (Tel: 2921 2669). The American Library (Tel: 2529 9661) in Admiralty has excellent research facilities.

SPORTING ACTIVITIES

Hong Kong's rugged and varied terrain as well as its coastal location make it an ideal spot for outdoor pursuits such as trail walking, cross country running and scuba diving. There is also plenty of scope for people who enjoy taking part in traditional sports such as football, tennis, bowls, cricket and squash. For the more adventurous there are parachuting, water-skiing and ice skating clubs. There are many scenic and challenging golf courses.

However, membership costs are often prohibitively high and places in some clubs are limited.

Hiking
Hong Kong is a fantastic place to go hiking and there are more than 20 country parks covering some 40 per cent of the Territory. There are some magnificent country walks just a few minutes out of the city and the views are truly spectacular. You will be able to buy maps of the major country trails at the Sale of Government Publications Office (Tel: 2523 5377) at the Main Post Office near the Star Ferry in Central. These trails are broken up into manageable stages so you will be able to decide in advance just how far you want to go, how long you want to take and how strenuous you want your walk to get. If you are determined to do a whole trail in one go don't forget your tent! The gruelling McLehose Trail alone runs for a hilly heart-breaking 60 miles through the New Territories.

Hashing
Hashing is an extremely popular form of running here. It is basically a glo-rified paper chase with one member of the group, the hare, setting a chalk trail for the rest, the pack, to follow. At the end of the run the hash mem-bers traditionally drink vast amounts of beer and then head off for a meal at one of the Territory's restaurants. There are several Hash House Harrier groups in Hong Kong – including the notorious men-only South Side. New members are always welcome and you may find this a very good way of getting to know people quickly. The Wanch pub on Jaffe Road in Wanchai is the spiritual home of the Hash runners and a list of the Hash clubs and the days on which they run can be found there.

Joining clubs
There are many sporting clubs and associations in Hong Kong catering to all tastes. Unfortunately, many of these have long waiting lists and it may be some time before you can become a full member. The facilities offered are normally very good. The best way of finding the club which will most suit you is by looking around at some and discussing the matter with friends and colleagues.

Major sporting occasions
For Hong Kong expatriates, the sporting event of the year is unquestionably the Hong Kong Rugby Sevens. Every spring thousands of rugby enthusi-asts come flying in from all corners of the globe to sample the action at the newly-renovated Government Stadium in Happy Valley. Most of the major rugby-playing nations send a team and the event has an atmosphere all of its own with wackily-dressed supporters, Mexican waves and busy beer tents all adding to the carnival feel.

Racing
Evening horse racing at Happy Valley and weekend racing at Shatin regularly draw vast crowds with gambling very much an established part of the Chinese way of life. The Formula Three Macau Grand Prix takes place in November when thousands of Hong Kong motor racing fans head across the water to the Portuguese enclave.

Tennis
International tennis tournaments regularly take place in Victoria Park, and some major running and golf tournaments at other venues throughout the Territory.

Football
There is a professional football league in Hong Kong which attracts some of the lesser known expatriate players. During the close season, a number of overseas clubs usually visit the Government Stadium to take on a Hong Kong team in an exhibition match.

Each year some new sporting extravaganza is drawn to Hong Kong where facilities are excellent and the crowds enthusiastic. The Hong Kong Cricket Sixes is quickly gaining an international reputation and you will also be able to enjoy some first-class squash, basketball, table tennis, Go-Kart racing and surfing action during the course of the year.

TOURIST ATTRACTIONS

Besides its natural attractions, the views from the Peak and across Victoria Harbour, Hong Kong has many interesting buildings and museums to visit. The Legco building was built in 1910 and the Governor's mansion is not far away and stands as a reminder of a long Colonial history. The Hong Kong Science Museum which opened in 1991 has some 500 exhibits and attracts nearly a million visitors annually. Extremely popular too is the distinctive domed Space Museum. The Hong Kong Museum of Art is located in the Cultural Centre in Tsimshatsui and features major collections of Chinese art, antiquities and pictures. The story of Hong Kong is told at the Hong Kong Museum of History in Kowloon Park with the help of archaeological finds and natural history exhibits.

Visiting temples
You will find lots of small colourful temples on both back streets and main streets all over the Territory. There are also several famous monuments which are definitely worth a look. The vast Ching Chung Koon Taoist temple, near Tuen Mun in the New Territories, is filled with many rooms con-

taining altars where prayers to the dead are made. The garden, with its fish ponds, pagodas, flowers and miniature trees, is as peaceful as it is pretty. Another popular spot is the Temple of the 10,000 Buddhas which is reached by climbing up about 500 steps in the hills of Shatin.

Other notable temples are the Man Mo Temple in Central, the Tin Hau Temple in Tin Hau, and the Wong Tai Sin Temple in Kowloon.

Exploring the public parks

Victoria Park in the heart of Causeway Bay has a dozen tennis courts, a jogging track, several outdoor hard-surface football pitches and an outdoor swimming pool. It is also popular with picnicking families and has a refreshments bar. Early in the morning you will find groups of people practising the ancient Chinese Tai Chi exercise movements here.

The expansive Hong Kong Park in Central houses an aviary, a massive greenhouse for tropical plants, a lake, restaurant, ampitheatre and a number of impressively-maintained gardens. The Kowloon Park in Tsimshatsui is another popular spot for picnickers, footballers and Tai Chi enthusiasts. There are numerous smaller gardens and parks in Hong Kong providing basketball courts, tennis courts, small lakes and ponds, but perhaps most importantly, benches and a chance to escape from the hustle and bustle of family life for a few minutes or a few hours.

Discovering the beaches

There are many sandy beaches lining Hong Kong's coastline but be warned, pollution here is a serious problem and many areas are heavily littered as well. The government leases and maintains some three dozen beaches and lifeguards are on duty during the summer months. Among the best beaches to visit are those at Deep Water Bay, Stanley, Repulse Bay, Big Wave Bay on Hong Kong Island, the Silverstrand Beach in the New Territories and the Tung Wa beach on Cheung Chau and Hung Shiung Yeh beach on Lamma.

CHECKLIST

● Use your time in Hong Kong to try a sport new to you.

● If you are hiking or hashing, remember not to overdo it and take plenty of water with you.

CASE STUDIES

David finds plenty to do

'Rebecca and I have both been really impressed with the standard of shows which come here. We used to go to a lot of theatre at home and we're really keen to broaden our cultural horizons while we're here and to get a feel for Asian style entertainment. The Hong Kong Museum of Art was a real eye opener and helped us to appreciate the sheer age of Chinese civilisation. We're hoping to get around a lot of the temples as well so I don't think we're going to be short of things to do at the weekends.'

Sarah gets the hang of shopping

'Well, "shop till you drop" is exactly what I have been doing. I love it. I could just spend all day everyday poking round the markets and street stalls and I'm really into the haggling and all that. I reckon I'm getting pretty good at it too. I can't believe how many stores there are here. It's just as well I haven't got a credit card yet!'

Tony gets hooked on hashing

'Apparently there are lots of countries where this hashing business is done but I'd never heard of it before. I'm certainly a convert now. I run with the South Side on a Thursday night and it's a real laugh. I've met loads of good blokes – a real mixture from all walks of life. We're planning a hash outing to Macau in a couple of weeks so I've been saving up a bit for that. Apparently it can get a bit wild so they've all warned me to be prepared for anything. We'll see!'

DISCUSSION POINTS

1. Are you aware of all of the major sporting and cultural events coming to Hong Kong in the next few months?

2. Have you made a list of all the things you would really like to do while you are in Hong Kong?

12
Holidaying in the Region

Hong Kong is an ideal base from which to explore the many mysteries of the Asian region. It has excellent air links with nearly all of its neighbours and you will find yourself within a few hours flying time of such exotic destinations as Thailand, Malaysia, the Philippines, Japan, Singapore, Indonesia and even Vietnam and Burma. But despite the sandy beaches, clear blue water and golden sun on offer in these countries, it is China, Hong Kong's giant neighbour to the north, which may well be your first 'overseas' destination.

Getting away

For travel to some Asian countries you may well require more extensive **immunisations** than were administered prior to your arrival in Hong Kong. For further information on the medical requirements of travel to your particular destination consult your doctor or the Port Health Inoculation Centres in Wanchai (Tel: 2572 2056) or Yaumatei (Tel: 2368 3361). Before taking a trip, it is sensible to get yourself proper **travel insurance** covering such eventualities as ill health or theft of your personal goods. This can be arranged through most Hong Kong travel agents.

In the majority of countries in south-east Asia, the **US dollar** is the preferred foreign currency and it is well worth taking some small notes with you. **Traveller's cheques** can be obtained in all major banks in Hong Kong and it is probably wise to have these made out in American dollars also.

Regular air-conditioned airport buses run to and from Kai Tak International Airport from a number of locations. Depending on how many of you are travelling together this will probably work out cheaper than taking a taxi and is often more convenient.

You will pay a relatively small departure tax when flying from Hong Kong. This will be paid as you check in for your flight.

VISITING CHINA

Crossing from Hong Kong to China is a simple affair and, although **visas** are required, these can be quickly obtained. The simplest way to arrange a trip is through one of the offices of the China Travel Service (Tel: 2721 1331). There are a number of different kinds of visas available ranging from a one-day single entry visa to a six-month multiple entry. When crossing the border into the mainland it is no longer necessary to fill in endless forms and there is a simple entry and departure card to complete. Travelling to China has never been easier and the level of tourism is finally beginning to reach the same heights that it had prior to the Tiananmen Square massacre in 1989.

Getting there

You can now travel across into China by virtually every mode of transport invented. If you are planning a visit to Beijing then you will almost certainly choose to travel by plane but there are a whole host of fascinating places to see a lot closer to 'home'. The Shenzhen Special Economic Zone is just a stone's throw from the Territory's outer reaches and has become a major manufacturing and business centre for Hong Kong people. Trains run between Hong Kong and Shenzhen via Lo Wu frequently throughout the day. The travelling time of 40 minutes is often considerably lengthened by the cross-border checking procedures. You may also catch a bus from various points in Hong Kong or catch a ferry to Shekou. If you wish to explore other areas of Guangdong's Pearl River Delta, ferries and hydrofoils run frequently from Hong Kong to Zhuhai and Zhongshan and you may travel to the port of Guangzhou, otherwise known as Canton, by ferry, train or air.

Shenzhen

This rambling city of two million people is said to be Communist China's answer to Hong Kong. In 1980 this teeming metropolis was a sleepy fishing village. Then, China's paramount leader Deng Xiaoping declared it a special economic zone and offered tax breaks and other incentives for foreign investors to come here. The overseas cash came, most of it from Hong Kong, and giant industrial complexes sprung up alongside five-star hotels and restaurants. Impoverished peasants from across China flooded to this new 'paradise' in the hope of a better life. They now supply the cheap labour which pumps out cheap manufactured goods such as toys and teddy bears for sale in the west. They work in cramped conditions and often live in workers' dorms next to the factory.

Crime and corruption
Despite a series of government crackdowns, corruption in the city remains rife and crime continues to skyrocket. Prostitutes patrol the streets and child beggars line the pavements. Shenzhen is a glitzy city, devoid of soul, lacking in culture or style, and yet still it works. For all the poverty and all the hardship you see, you will see also the trappings of wealth and success.

Mercedes alongside pushbikes, achievement alongside hope. Shenzhen has its dark side and yet for most of the 'exploited' workers life in the factories is infinitely better than it was in the paddy fields of their home provinces.

Shenzhen boasts a number of theme parks which attracts the tourists. Among these are Splendid China, which includes a model of the Great Wall, China Folk Culture Village and Window of the World which recreates a host of landmarks from across the globe. Shenzhen is not an accurate reflection of what the real China is like but it does provide an insight into what some would like the real China to be. You will find a visit here fascinating.

The Pearl River Delta
Most people from Hong Kong visit the historic port of Guangzhou for business purposes although the city does have a number of interesting museums, statues and memorial parks. The Zhuhai Special Economic Zone, like Shenzhen, was set up in 1980 and, like Shenzhen, it has proved an economic success story. It also caters to the many tourists who pop across the border from nearby Macau, most of whom take a walk around the gardens in the Zhuhai Resort. The Zhongshang region is a fertile and flourishing district of the Pearl River Delta which supplies Macau with most of its fresh produce. A number of new industries have also moved into the area, helping to guarantee its future prosperity.

Beijing
China's capital city is something of a showcase for the People's Republic. You may be amazed by its cleanliness and, above all, its wealth. Beijing is absolutely packed with first-class hotels, delicious eateries and breathtaking sights. It also skilfully mixes the old and the new: McDonald's burger bars and the Forbidden City, Chinese opera and disco dancing. This ancient city has changed quickly in recent years and is now a pleasant posting for overseas diplomats and businessmen. It is also very tourist-friendly and the independent traveller will find little trouble exploring the mystery of Beijing on his or her own. There are pre-arranged tours of China's capital city available in Hong Kong, although you may prefer to simply buy your flights in the Territory and sort out your own itinerary once you arrive. There is no shortage of things to see and do.

Top sightseeing spots in Beijing
Tiananmen Square
Sadly, the spiritual heart of the Chinese capital is now most famous as the venue where the 1989 pro-democracy movement was brutally crushed. There is little indication today that the massacre ever happened. Young children fly kites, street vendors sell drinks and ice creams, Chinese

families laugh and joke and take photographs of each other. Although you may spot the odd policeman mingling with the crowds, a calm normality has long since returned to Tiananmen. Surrounding the square are a variety of monuments including the Great Hall of the People, the Mao Mausoleum, the Monument to the People's Heros and the Gate of Heavenly Peace on which hangs a huge portrait of Chairman Mao.

Forbidden City
Originally built early in the 15th century the Forbidden City was the place from where the ancient emperors ruled China. For some five centuries it was forbidden for all but an exclusive group to enter the city – hence the name. There is a separate entry point – and price – for foreigners and Chinese wishing to visit the Forbidden City. The admission price will entitle you to an audio-cassette guide which explains the history and the significance of all the buildings and carvings.

Summer Palace
About twelve kilometres out of the city centre, this vast and beautiful park is where the emperors used to spend the summer months away from the Forbidden City. The Kunming Lake occupies 75 per cent of the park which contains numerous gardens and beauty spots. There are a number of temples and interesting architectural features. The beautifully-embellished Long Corridor is 700 metres long.

The Great Wall
The Great Wall of China can comfortably be visited on a day trip from Beijing. This incredible piece of construction, which is the only man-made structure on earth which can be seen from outer space, was started during the Qing Dynasty some 2,000 years ago in order to protect the ancient kingdoms. Most excursions from Beijing will take you to see the Wall at Badaling. **A must see.**

ENJOYING MACAU

The tiny Portuguese enclave of Macau is less than an hour away from Hong Kong by ferry or hydrofoil and is the perfect weekend retreat. There are scores of fascinating and atmospheric restaurants in which to while away an afternoon enjoying a reasonably-priced bottle of wine or two. There are even some very pleasant beaches as well. For the vast majority of visitors from Hong Kong, Macau's main attraction is its **casinos**. The booming gambling industry also means top-class hotels and top-class entertainment. The Formula Three Grand Prix is the big international event of the year and motor racing fans from across the world flock here every November.

Macau, which has a busy land border with China, also includes the islands of Taipa and Coloane and these are all linked by giant road bridges.

REST OF THE REGION

The proximity of the glorious beach resorts of Thailand and the Philippines is one of the major advantages of life in Hong Kong. Resorts such as Boracay, Koh Samui and Phuket, which are just a few hours' flight away, offer fantastic beaches, cheap food and accommodation and most importantly glorious sunshine. During Festival weekends or holiday times such as a Chinese New Year, these places will be packed with people from the Territory. Despite heavy development in many of the resorts and the growing presence of the tourist industry, the countries of south-east Asia have retained their individual character and unmistakable eastern flavour. You will find that the people are generally welcoming and friendly, but nonetheless it is only sensible to take reasonable care with personal belongings. It is worth remembering that cities such as Manila are among the poorest in the world.

Off the beaten track

If you are seeking to get off the beaten track, there are plenty of less touristy places to visit. Countries such as Vietnam, Burma and even Cambodia are just beginning to open up to overseas visitors and to overseas investors. News of the latest air fares and constantly-changing visa regulations are available from most of the many travel agents in Hong Kong. A number of travel books offer excellent guides to travel in this fascinating part of the world.

Countries and destinations within striking distance of Hong Kong

- China – Shenzhen, Pearl River Delta, Beijing

- Macau – Grand Prix Museum, Monte Fort, Coloane Park

- Taiwan – Taipei

- Thailand – Bangkok, Koh Samui, Chiang Mai

- Malaysia – Kuala Lumpar, Penang, Rantau Abang, Cherating

- Philippines – Manila, Boracay, Cebu, Palawan

- Vietnam – Ho Chi Minh City, Mekong Delta, Hanoi, Dalat

- Burma – Rangoon, Mandalay, Pagan, Pegu

- Cambodia – Pnomh Penh. Angkor, Battambang

- Japan – Tokyo, Kyoto, Osaka

- Indonesia – Bali, Sumatra, Kalimantan

- Nepal – Khatmandu, Mount Everest

- India – Delhi, Goa, Bombay, Jodphur.

Tips for explorers

- Take the ferry to Shenzhen and look around the city.

- Take a weekend break in Macau.

- Take a diving course in Hong Kong and plan a scuba holiday in the region.

- Ask friends and colleagues to recommend a good reasonably-priced travel agent.

CHECKLIST

- Make sure you have all the recommended immunisations for travelling in Asia.

- Decide which countries you *simply have to visit* while you are in Hong Kong.

- Make sure you are adequately insured for travelling in the region.

CASE STUDIES

David goes exploring

'Rebecca was very keen to go to China and having spent so much time in Shenzhen with my work, I wanted to go somewhere a bit further afield. We decided on Guangzhou and had a very pleasant journey on the overnight ferry from Tsimshatsui. Guangzhou was interesting although very crowded, and the best part of the trip was a cruise on the Pearl river. The children were horrified and excited by the Snake Restaurant in Guangzhou which had several serpents on display in the front window. I couldn't bring myself to indulge but Rebecca quite enjoyed the snake soup!'

Tony enjoys Macau

'I spent the weekend in Macau recently and I love the place. It was so much more relaxed than Hong Kong and the wine was really cheap too. I can't wait to go back. There's plenty to see as well and the views from the old fort are spectacular. The best thing is that it's only an hour or so away. And travel is so easy. It's hard to believe that you are actually going to another country.'

Sarah falls for Beijing

'We went up to Beijing for a long weekend but it wasn't long enough, believe me. We were expecting it to be quite rough and third-worldly but it wasn't like that at all. It was nice to get out to see the Great Wall but the tour we took only gave us about an hour there which was very disappointing. The Forbidden City was just out of this world and the gardens at the Summer Palace were truly beautiful.'

DISCUSSION POINTS

1. How easy will it be for you and your family to take time to explore neighbouring countries?

2. Are you prepared for the levels of poverty and deprivation that you might encounter?

13
Learning Cantonese

Cantonese is the language most commonly used in Hong Kong. However, Mandarin – also known as Putonghua – is the official language of the People's Republic of China and this is likely to become increasingly important. Both languages are tonal in nature, so it will help if you have a good ear. Although there is some disagreement about exactly how many tones there are in each language, Cantonese is generally considered to have six basic tones and Mandarin only four. Learning Chinese can prove particularly challenging because the same words spoken in a different tone often have a completely different meaning. It is quite possible to be extremely rude to someone without even trying! Be careful.

The good news about learning Chinese is that the grammar is exceptionally simple. There are no tenses, no articles and no plurals. This has the advantage of making it far easier to put basic sentences together very quickly. However, it also has the effect of making Chinese a very imprecise language so more words need to be spoken to make the exact meaning clear.

Communicating in pictures
While there are many different spoken Chinese dialects there is only one written form of the language. This helps to make communication between Chinese people much easier. Chinese characters are basically small pictures which can involve a dozen or more pen strokes. To learn to read and write Chinese is a massive undertaking and will involve incredible patience and perseverance. There are thousands of characters to memorise even to attain a basic reading ability. If you are serious about having a go at mastering written Chinese don't underestimate the size of your task.

CHOOSING A COURSE

There are many excellent Cantonese and, to a lesser extent, Mandarin courses available in the Territory. Many larger companies are now offering their employees the opportunity to attend Mandarin classes, but for the most part these are intended for Cantonese speakers. Courses are run at some English Schools Foundation schools in the evening, at the universities and also by the YMCA or YWCA. If you are looking for a **private tutor**, scan through the classified sections in the English language press. Another alternative is to try and learn the language yourself by buying a book or an audio-cassette course. If you have the time and the will it is quite possible to make good progress in this manner.

PRACTISING PRONUNCIATION

The key to learning any language, of course, is lots of practice and you should not be afraid to use your new language skills at the shops, in the restaurant, or in the workplace. If you have audio tapes to practise with at home, all well and good. Try to set aside a certain amount of time each day to listen to the tapes and to repeat the words and tones over and over again – while you take the dog out or while you are walking to the MTR station, for example.

You must overcome any reluctance to try out your Cantonese on the local population. It is the only real way to know if you are making progress and to discover where you are going wrong. Go to your local supermarket and ask one of the shop assistants where the sugar is, go to a street market and ask for some cabbage, tell your taxi driver when to turn left and right and try and chat to your Chinese colleagues at work. You will find that people will respond to you in a far more positive manner if you demonstrate that you are at least making an effort to learn their language. They will probably also take great delight in the fact that you are finding it so difficult!

CHECKLIST

- As you start to learn a few words of Cantonese, listen out for them when you're sitting on the MTR or standing in a tram queue.

- Start to use a few simple phrases regularly even if it is Jo san or Nei ho ma? It will help to build confidence.

- Buy a new exercise book and make a note of all the new words and phrases you have learned.

- Set aside a certain period every day as your language studying time.

CASE STUDIES

David is learning Mandarin
'I'm getting on quite well with my Mandarin course. My company has very

Cantonese

Jo san	Good morning
Nei ho ma?	How are you?
Gei ho	Quite good
M'goi	Thank you (for a service)
Doh je	Thank you (for a gift)
Ngoh hai Ying Gwok yan	I am an Englishman
Kui hai mae Gwok Yan	She is American
Kui hai Jung Gwok man, m'hai?	Is she Chinese?
Gei do Cheen?	How much is it?
Tie gwoo why	Too expensive
Jaaw hoy	Go away
M'sai	There's no need

Mandarin

Ni hau	Hello
Wo tingbudong	I don't understand
Wo yau qu	I want to go
Cesuo	Toilet
Duoshao qian?	How much is it?
Tai guile	Too expensive
Wo milule	I'm lost
Mingtian	Tomorrow

Fig. 10. A few common Chinese phrases.

much encouraged me to learn the language and it's coming . . . slowly. I think it would be a lot easier to learn Cantonese because most of the people on the street speak it and it would be nice to be able to listen. Having said that I'm spending more and more of my time over the border now and I really feel like I can conquer this thing.'

Tony practises his Cantonese

'I've been picking up a fair bit of Cantonese and am really making an effort. Some guy who I met who was leaving Hong Kong gave me these cassettes and books on learning the language and they've really helped. I think you get a really different reaction from people on the streets when you buy things using Cantonese or get into a little conversation with them. It makes you stand out from the other Westerners here. Like you're sort of becoming a local. It's cool.'

Sarah runs into difficulties

'Don't talk to me about Cantonese. It's driving me crazy. I've been doing this course two nights a week at one of the schools and I just don't seem to be getting anywhere with it. I think it's the tones that get me, I guess I just haven't got the ear for it. I think I'll stick to the course and maybe do one more term. I'm never going to be a fluent Cantonese speaker but it would be nice if I were able to impress my friends when I go back to the States by ordering a few dishes at the local Chinese restaurant.'

DISCUSSION POINTS

1. Would you be better to learn Cantonese or Mandarin?

2. What basic words or phrases would be most useful for you to know?

14
1997 and Beyond

The fate of Hong Kong after the Chinese takeover of 30 June 1997 has been the subject of immense international speculation for decades. Perhaps not even the Chinese themselves are sure what the future holds for the Territory. Events are shaped by the personalities of those in power and by the circumstances in which they operate – both of which can change without a moment's notice.

You might understandably be wary about living in a place surrounded by so much uncertainty. However, much of this is due to the historic uniqueness of Hong Kong's situation. There is certainly no reason to believe that China would deliberately want to damage the vibrancy and success of Hong Kong and, therefore, it is hard to believe that the Territory is suddenly going to turn from being a fantastic place to live into one which is not. It will be many years before one can say with any confidence exactly what impact the transfer of sovereignty will have had. What can be stated with confidence is that it is in everyone's interests that Hong Kong continues to thrive and to prosper.

DOING BUSINESS ACROSS THE BORDER

The fate of Hong Kong has always been inextricably linked to that of its giant neighbour to the north. This has never been more evident than since 1980 when Deng Xiaoping's economic reforms brought a flood of overseas investment into China's newly-established special economic zones. The lure of tax allowances and cheap labour has prompted 60 per cent of Hong Kong manufacturers to move just across the border. There are said to be some 50,000 Hong Kong-owned companies in the Pearl River area and around 150,000 Hong Kong nationals earn their living in the Shenzhen Special Economic Zone alone. Whatever your field, there is a very good chance that your company will have direct dealings with China and many expatriates are required to make regular trips across the border in the course of their work.

The impact of all this investment and manufacturing is reflected in the prosperity of the local population. Shenzhen residents enjoy the highest monthly salaries in China, some 50 per cent higher than workers living in Beijing. However, investors are already heading further north into China in search of even cheaper rents and even cheaper labour. This trend is likely to be exacerbated in the coming years.

Although China's flourishing special economic zones are unlikely ever to rival Hong Kong's preeminent economic position, their importance is set to increase as cross-border links continue to strengthen and financial and business cooperation grows.

CHINA'S PROMISES

Under the Joint Declaration signed by Britain and China in 1984 the entire territory of Hong Kong will be handed over to China at midnight on 30 June 1997. Under the terms of the deal China made a number of specific promises relating to the future of the former colony. Hong Kong, it said, would become a Special Administrative Region of China and, as such, would maintain a high degree of autonomy – except in the fields of foreign affairs and defence – for at least 50 years. Although top-level British officials will leave, they will not be replaced by men from the mainland. Instead, Hong Kong people are to be allowed to govern themselves and, according to the Joint Declaration, the Territory's executive, legislative and judicial system would remain basically in place.

A number of guarantees were issued relating to the social and economic systems under which the individual's freedom of speech, assembly and travel were protected. China also promised to allow the free flow of capital and to ensure that the Hong Kong dollar would remain in circulation and would be fully convertible. Beijing also said it would not levy taxes on the Special Administrative Region. The maintenance of pubic order would be left in the hands of the Hong Kong government.

The terms of the agreement
The agreement ensures:

● existing trade and economic systems will continue

● free movement of goods and capital

● English common law system will be retained

● fundamental human rights will be protected by law

● freedom of movement to and from the Territory

● independence of the judiciary

● Hong Kong dollar will remain freely convertible

● Hong Kong's autonomy guaranteed in conduct of external commercial relations.

The signing of the Joint Declaration was greeted with a mixture of suspicion, resignation and guarded optimism in Hong Kong. However, this was to change four years later when Chinese troops brutally crushed the fledgling pro-democracy movement in Tiananmen Square.

PATTEN'S REFORMS

The arrival of Governor Chris Patten in Hong Kong sparked genuine excitement. Here was a man who had the ear of the British Prime Minister. A skilled and adept politician with popular appeal who could reflect and interpret the fears and desires of Hong Kong people. Governor Patten introduced a package of political reforms designed to increase the levels of democracy in the Territory. For some in Hong Kong, the reforms did not go far enough, for others they went too far. Predictably, Beijing was outraged and launched a series of vitriolic attacks against Mr Patten. As relations deteriorated, the Governor's reforms were approved by the Territory's legislators and subsequent local elections have resulted in wins for the democracy parties. However, turnouts were relatively low.

Legislative council elections

Figure 11 shows how the way in which the members of the Legislative Council are chosen has changed in the past decade.

	1984	1985	1988	1991	1995
Appointed	29	22	20	18	–
Ex Officio/Official	18	10	10	3	–
* Elected by Electoral College	–	12	12	–	–
Elected by Geographical Constituency	–	–	–	18	20
Elected by Functional Constituency	–	12	14	21	30
** Elected by Election Committee	–	–	–	–	10
Total	47	56	56	60	60

Fig. 11. The composition of the Legislative Council.

*All members of district boards and municipal councils
** All elected members of district boards

The new democratic nature of Governor Patten's model for the Legislative Council was put to the test on 17 September 1995, with the Legco Elections. Altogether 920,000 voters cast their votes in the geographical elections which returned 20 members. In total, more than 170,000 extra people cast their ballot than the 750,000 who have done so in the previous elections in 1991. The turnout rate was 35.8 per cent. The Democratic Party and its close allies won a total of 30 seats, the pro-China camp secured 15 seats, the Liberal Party ten seats and 'neutral' independents the other five. The Hong Kong government wasted no time in declaring the elections a resounding success but those in power to the north were dismissing the poll as 'irrelevant'.

China's fury

Beijing has been infuriated by Patten's political reforms and has effectively vowed to scrap the Legislative Council and set up its own provisional legislature at the earliest possible opportunity. In January 1996, China officially appointed a Preparatory Committee which was given the task of determining how Hong Kong will be governed after the transfer of sovereignty. Just 94 of the committee's 150-strong members came from Hong Kong, and perhaps, more significantly, none of them belonged to the Democratic Party. The Preparatory Committee will appoint a selection committee to set up an interim appointed legislature to take over from the elected Legislative Council the moment sovereignty is handed over.

For many, the acrimonious dispute over Patten's political reforms has been a confirmation of their worst fears. The much-desired smooth transfer of power has been disrupted and cooperation on other issues has suffered as a result of worsening Sino-British relations.

POLITICAL UNCERTAINTY

China's anger at Patten's political reforms naturally heightened fears about the transfer of sovereignty. The dispute has helped to 'politicise' the people of Hong Kong. After many years of concentrating on ways of making money against the stable background of British colonial administration, people now want to have their say. Political parties have been reformed, rallies have been held, protests made. This sort of activity is unlikely to be viewed positively by a government which ordered troops onto Tianenmen Square. But the Chinese takeover raises other concerns to.

Corruption

Corruption, for so long a major problem in Hong Kong, has been brought under some sort of control by the activities of the Independent Commission against Corruption. If serious corruption were again to rear its ugly head under Chinese sovereignty, there are real fears that it could create sufficient instability and uncertainty to deter overseas investment. There is considerable concern also about the fact that troops of the People's Liberation Army will be visibly garrisoned in Hong Kong.

Intervention

China has promised it will not intervene in the running of the Territory, but is that a realistic prospect? Most people think it is not a matter of if, but to what extent they will interfere with Hong Kong's government. The sceptics point to the presidential elections held in Taiwan in early 1996 when China blatantly tried to intimidate the voters of the island by conducting war games off its coast. In Hong Kong this action fuelled alarm over the takeover and disturbances were reported as thousands of people scrambled to beat the deadline to obtain British travel documents.

Not even massive investment in projects such as the new HK$159 billion Chep Lap Kok Airport and the HK$10 billion container terminal at Kwang Chai have been sufficient to convince everyone that Hong Kong will retain its status as Asia's centre of trade and travel.

Emigration

Emigration is, of course, the Hong Kong people's ultimate vote of no confidence in Chinese rule and many people have acquired foreign passports as insurance against a decline in the Territory's prosperity. Surveys suggest that nearly three-quarters of a million Hong Kong residents hold foreign passports and two million more have families abroad which would sponsor them if they were to choose to leave. Canada is the most popular choice followed by Australia, the United States and New Zealand (see Figure 12). Between 1988 and 1995, a total of 434,000 people emigrated from the Territory. However, it is estimated that, having obtained foreign passports, at least 12 per cent of those who left have since returned to Hong Kong.

LOWERING THE UNION JACK

When the Union Flag is lowered from Government House for the last time, it will represent the symbolic end of a long and lucrative British stewardship of the Territory. However, a large British community will remain, some members of which have lived in the Territory for most of their lives. British business interests are naturally well established and many trade associations and professional bodies have strong UK links. The civil service has been undergoing a localisation process for a number of years and although the influence of British training and administration methods may long remain, the presence of British personnel will not. Some UK civil servants are eligible to continue in their posts having satisfied a number of

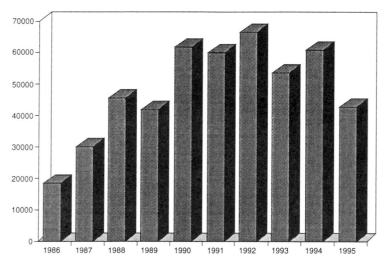

Fig. 12. Estimated emigration figures 1986-1995.

language and residency criteria, but they will be downgraded from expatriate to local terms and in some cases will have reduced responsibility. While the wealth and vibrancy of Hong Kong will continue to attract adventurous and opportunity-seeking expatriates, there is a feeling that things will never quite be the same again.

The Doomsday scenario

In the Joint Declaration, Beijing has promised that Hong Kong will retain its autonomy in the commercial field for at least 50 years. So what could go wrong? Put simply, there are few people who think that China will be able to resist tinkering with the system? Will it really allow demonstrations to take place? How will it react to criticism from the people of Hong Kong? What will be the political fallout from its dismantling of the democratically-elected legislative machinery?

The doomsday scenario could be described as one in which China becomes increasingly involved in the minutiae of the Territory's affairs and by doing so makes small problems worse. The intrinsic heavy handedness and lack of political skill of the authorities in Beijing will only serve to damage confidence in Hong Kong. This could trigger with withdrawal of multinational business to other regional centres followed by widescale emigration and a mounting sense of panic. The permanent relocation of skilled professionals would undermine the social infrastructure and corruption and crime could become rife.

Thankfully, such a scenario is unlikely ever to come about, simply because there are too many vested interests in making sure that it doesn't.

'It would not be realistic to think of an agreement that provides for continued British administration in Hong Kong after 1997.'

Sir Geoffrey Howe (former British foreign secretary), April 20 1984

'In terms of reunification, the return of Hong Kong to the motherland is the first station in our long march. After that there is Macau and finally Taiwan.'

China's President Jiang Zemin, January 1996

'Our proposal for two systems to be practised in one country has taken into full consideration the actual conditions in Hong Kong. I believe that the people of Hong Kong have the ability to administer Hong Kong. The Chinese are by no means short of talent.'

China's paramount leader, Deng Xiaoping, June 1984

'This is a black day for democracy in Hong Kong. A Chinese government-appointed body of Chinese government officials and hand-picked Hong Kong advisers has voted to tear down a legislature which was freely, fairly and openly elected by the people of Hong Kong in the most democratic election in our history.'

Governor Chris Patten, March 1996

Fig. 13. They said it about Hong Kong.

The hypothetical situation does, however, serve as a warning of just how much of a tightrope Hong Kong is now walking. Confidence is everything. If anything were to shake that confidence, the consequences are potentially catastrophic.

The tail wagging the dog

Once you have paid a visit to Shenzhen or one of the other special economic zones across the border in the People's Republic of China you will begin to appreciate why many are convinced that it is not so much a case of China taking over Hong Kong as the other way around. Businessmen who have moved their manufacturing base across the border see the liberalisation of China's economic policies as an exciting opportunity and they view 1997 in the same way. It is widely felt that the economic might and deal-making know-how of the Territory and its population will ensure that it is Beijing which will be seeking the advice and help rather than vice-versa.

The wealth of the Territory was forged in the competitive world of international commerce and China is desperate to increase its competitiveness in the marketplace. If Beijing can demonstrate to the world that it can be trusted to guard the prosperity and well-being of such a rich prize as Hong Kong then further overseas investment can be expected to flood into the whole of southern China.

This optimistic model is, of course, dependent on no major political crises, that China truly does allow one country two systems to operate and that the cream of Hong Kong's entrepreneurial talent elects not to emigrate. It is, perhaps, in the hands and abilities of these deal-making ambitious individuals in which the Territory's fate truly lies.

PROSPECTS FOR EXPATRIATES

There is little real doubt that Hong Kong will remain a fantastic place for expatriates to live and work. Wages are likely to remain high, leisure facilities to remain excellent and crime levels to remain low. The presence of Western residents is highly reassuring to the local population and offers proof that it really is 'business as usual' in Hong Kong. China is therefore anxious not to do anything which might prompt a sudden decampment. While the golden days of Hong Kong may be over as far as the expatriate civil servant is concerned, for you and your family they are most probably just beginning.

CASE STUDIES

David dismisses the doomsday theory

'I really find all of this talk of doom and gloom in Hong Kong about 1997 most amusing. To read some of the British papers you would think the end of the world was nigh. You only have to take a walk down the street to know that that is not the case. Buildings are still going up like crazy, people are making long-term business commitments and look at all of the Hong Kong investment in manufacturing across the border. People here aren't going anywhere. There's enough money to be made and enough deals to be done right here. I know my company for one is looking forward to finding new markets in the PRC as that country continues to open up.'

Tony has no reservations

'I can understand why people who don't understand China might think that they will make a mess of things in Hong Kong, but why should they? The success of the special economic zones is proof that Beijing is serious about reform. I certainly have no reservations about staying here and none of my friends does either. Besides, we can leave any time we like.'

Sarah thinks little will change

'I can't say I'm too thrilled about living in Communist China all of a sudden. My dad thinks I'm absolutely crazy for wanting to stay, but why not. Even if things do change for the worse it's going to take ages and ages to happen. Chinese troops aren't suddenly going to appear on the streets declaring martial law or something. That's just ridiculous.'

DISCUSSION POINTS

1. What are your options if at any stage you decide that Hong Kong is no longer a place in which you wish to bring up your family?

2. Look for the positive aspects of Chinese sovereignty – what business opportunities does it offer?

Keep abreast of political changes and events.
You are helping to shape history. Enjoy it.

Useful Addresses

The following list details some addresses and telephone numbers which you may find useful. It is not a comprehensive guide to all the facilities and companies available under each category, but simply provides a base from which to work.

GENERAL

Hong Kong Tourist Association, Shop 8, Basement Jardine House, 1 Connaught Place, Central. Hotline: 2801 7177. (Also offices at Kai Tak Airport and Star Ferry Terminal at Tsimshatsui).

Hong Kong Government Information Services, G/F, 1/f, 4/F, 5/F & 6/F Beaconsfield House, 4 Queens Road, Central. Tel: 2842 8777.

Registration of Persons Office, Hong Kong Office, 8th Floor, Immigration Tower, 7 Gloucester Road, Wanchai. Tel: 2824 6111.

Registration of Persons Office, Kowloon Office, 2nd Floor, Empire Centre, 68 Mody Road, Tsimshatsui. Tel: 2368 0479.

Registration of Persons Office, Tsuen Wan Office, Level 4, Tseun Wan Ferry Pier, Tsuen Wan Waterfront, Tseun Wan. Tel: 2498 4242.

Sale of Government Publications Office, G/FL GPO Building, Central. Tel: 2523 5377.

Consumer Council, China Hong Kong City, Canton Road, Tsimshatsui. Tel: 2736 3636.

Rent-a-Mum (babysitting service), 88B Pokfulam Road, Hong Kong. Tel: 2817 9799.

Port Health Information Centre, 2/F Centre Point Building, 181-185 Gloucester Road, Wanchai. Tel: 2572 2056.

Port Health Inoculation Centre, Rm 905 Government Offices, Canton Road, Yaumatei, Kowloon, Tel: 2368 3361.

BUSINESS AND CHAMBERS OF COMMERCE

Business Registration Office, Inland Revenue Department, 3/F Windsor House, 311 Gloucester Road, Causeway Bay. Tel: 2894 3149.

Hong Kong Trade Development Council, 38/F Office Tower, Convention Plaza, 1 Harbour Road. Tel: 2833 4333.

Inland Revenue Dept, Windsor House, 311 Gloucester Road, Causeway Bay. Tel: 2894 5098.

Hong Kong Chamber of Commerce, 902 Swire House, 9-25 Chater Road, Central. Tel: 2523 7177.

American Chamber of Commerce, 10/F Swire House, Central. Tel: 2526 0165.

British Chamber of Commerce, 6/F 8 Queens Road, Central. Tel: 2810 8118.

EMBASSIES

Australian Embassy, 23/F & 24/F Harbour Centre, 25 Harbour Road, Wanchai. Tel: 2827 8881.

Canadian Embassy, 11/F-14/F Tower One, Exchange Square, 8 Connaught Place, Central. Tel: 2810 4321.

Chinese Consulate, Visa office of the Ministry of Foreign Affairs, 5/F Lower Block, 26 Harbour Road, Wanchai. Tel: 2835 3794.

American Embassy, 26 Garden Road, Central. Tel: 2523 9011.

EMPLOYMENT AGENCIES

Drake Employment Agency, 18/F Peregrine Tower, Lippo Centre, Drake Street. Tel: 2848 9288.

Staff Service, 15/F Shell Tower, Times Square, 1 Matheson Street, Causeway Bay. Tel: 2506 2676.

Global Employment, 9/F HK Pacific Centre, 28 Hankow Road, Tsimshatsui. Tel: 2731 3676.

Sarah Beattie Employment Agency, Sung Hung Kai Centre, 3/F 30 Harbour Road, Wanchai. Tel: 2507 9333.

Webster Employment Agency, 1004 Lane Crawford House, 70 Queen's Road, Central. Tel: 2845 6116.

ENTERTAINMENT VENUES

Hong Kong Coliseum, 9 Cheong Wan Road, Hunghom, Kowloon. Tel: 2355 7234.

Queen Elizabeth Stadium, 18 Oi Kwan Road, Wanchai. Tel: 2591 7234.

Hong Kong Cultural Centre, 10 Salisbury Road, Tsimshatsui. Tel: 2734 2009.

City Hall, Edinburgh Place, Central. Tel: 2921 2840.

Hong Kong Science Museum, 2 Science Museum Road, Tsimshatsui. Tel: 2732 3232.

PRIVATE HOSPITALS

Hong Kong Adventist Hospital, 40 Stubbs Road. Tel: 2574 6211.
Hong Kong Baptist Hospital, 222 Waterloo Road. Tel: 2339 8888.
Matilda & War Memorial Hospital, 41 Mt Kellett Road, The Peak. Tel:
2849 6301.

BUDGET ACCOMMODATION

Park Guesthouse, 15/F A Block, Chunking Mansions, Tsimshatsui. Tel:
2368 1689.
Garden Guesthouse, 7/F C Block, Chungking Mansions. Tel: 2368 7414.
Regent Guesthouse. 6/F E Block, Chungking Mansions. Tel: 2722 0833.
Man Hing Lung Guesthouse, 14/F Mirador Arcade, 58 Nathan Road,
Tsimshatsui. Tel: 2722 0678.
Star Guesthouse, 6/F 21 Cameron Road, Tsimshatsui. Tel: 273 8951.
Noble Guesthouse, Flat C1 7/F, 37 Paterson St, Causeway Bay. Tel: 2576
6148.
Emerald House Guesthouse, 44 Leighton Road, Causeway Bay. Tel: 2577
2368.

INSURANCE COMPANIES

East Asia/ Aetna Insurance Group, 10/F City Plaza 4, Taikoo Shing. Tel:
2513 3888. Travel Insurance Tel: 2544 0321.
Eagle Star Life Insurance, Level 18, One Pacific Place, 88 Queensway. Tel:
2810 0313.
Swire Insurance, Swire House. Tel: 2840 8080.
Cigna Worldwide Insurance, East Point Centre. Tel: 2833 9929.

EDUCATION

Education Department, Wu Chung House 16/F, 213 Queen's Road East,
Wanchai, Hong Kong.
The English Schools Foundation, 43B Stubbs Road, Hong Kong. Tel: 2574
2351.

English Schools Foundation

Junior schools
Beacon Hill Junior School, 23 Ede Road, Kowloon Tong, Kowloon. Tel:
2336 5221.
Bradbury Junior School, 43C Stubbs Road, Hong Kong. Tel: 2574 8240.

Clearwater Bay School, DD229, Lot 235, Clearwater Bay Road, Kowloon. Tel: 2358 3221.

Glenealy Junior School, 7 Hornsey Road, Mid-Levels, Hong Kong. Tel: 2522 1919.

Kennedy School: 19 Sha Wan Drive, Pokfulam, Hong Kong. Tel: 2855 0711.

Kowloon Junior School, 20 Perth Street, Kowloon. Tel: 2714 5279.

Peak School, 20 Plunketts Road, The Peak, Hong Kong. Tel: 2849 7211.

Quarry Bay Junior School, 6 Hau Yuen Path, Braemar Hill, Hong Kong. Tel: 2566 4242.

Shatin Junior School, 3A Lai Wo Lane, Fo Tan, Sha Tin, NT. Tel: 2692 2721.

Secondary schools

Island School, 20 Borrett Road, Hong Kong. Tel: 2524 7135.

King George V School, 2 Tin Kwong Road, Homantin, Kowloon. Tel: 2711 3028.

Shatin College, 3 Lai Wo Lane, Fo Tan, Sha Tin, NT. Tel: 2699 1811.

South Island School, 50 Nam Fung Road, Hong Kong. Tel: 2555 9314.

West Island School, 250 Victoria Road, Pokfulam, Hong Kong. Tel: 2819 1962.

Private schools offering British curriculum

Chinese International School, Hau Yuen Path, Braemar Hill, IL, 8743, North Point, Hong Kong. Tel: 2510 7288.

Delia Memorial School, 221 Hip Wo Street, Kwun Tong, Kowloon. Tel: 2342 3175.

Discovery Bay International School, Discovery Bay, Lantau Island. Tel: 2987 7331.

Kellett School, 2 Wah Lok Path, Phase 1 Stage 1 Part of G-3/F, Wah Fu Estate, Hong Kong. Tel: 2551 8234.

Royden House Junior and Senior School, 110 Caine Road, Mid-Levels, Hong Kong. Tel: 2547 5479.

Sears Rigers International School, 109 Boundary Street, Kowloon (primary) and 14 & 55 Cumberland Road, Kowloon (secondary). Tel: 2339 1612 or 2336 5438.

German Swiss International School, 11 Guildford Road, The Peak, Hong Kong. Tel: 2849 6216.

The Hong Lok Yuen International School, 3 Twentieth Street, Hong Lok Yuen, Tai Po, NT. Tel: 2658 6935.

Yew Cheung International School, 7 Selkirk Road (kindergarten), 2 Kent Road, Kowloon Tong (primary), 11-13 Kent Road (secondary). Tel: 2336 5231, 2338 8774 or 2336 3443.

Private schools offering American/Canadian curriculum

California International (USA) School, 143 Waterloo Road, G/F-1/F, Kowloon Tong and 123 and 125 Waterloo Road, Kowloon Tong. Tel: 2304 5077 or 2336 3812.

Canadian International School, 7 Eastern Hospital Road, Hong Kong. Tel: 2881 0344.

Delia School of Canada, Po Shan Mansion, Tower T-11, G/F and 4/F, Tai Koo Shing, Quarry Bay, Hong Kong. Tel: 2884 4165.

Concordia International School, 68 Begonia Road, G/F to 3F and Room 301, Yau Yat Chuen, Kowloon. Tel: 2397 6576.

SEA Canadian Overseas Secondary School, 166-166A Boundary Street, G/F-2/F, Kowloon Tong and 121 Boundary Street, Kowloon Tong, Kowloon. Tel: 2336 1116.

The Hong Kong International School, South Bay Close, Repulse Bay, Hong Kong and Red Hill, Tai Tam, Hong Kong. Tel: 2612 2305.

Christian Alliance P.C. Lau Memorial College, 2 Fu Hing Street, Ma Tau Chung Road, Kowloon. Tel: 2713 3253.

International Christian School, 45-47 Grampian Road, Hong Kong. Tel: 2338 9606.

Private schools offering other curriculum

Lycée Française International, 34 Price Road, Jardine's Lookout, Hong Kong. Tel: 2577 6217.

The German Swiss International School, 11 Guildford Road, The Peak, Hong Kong. Tel: 2849 6216.

Singapore International School, 12 Ka Wai Man Road, Kennedy Town, Hong Kong. Tel: 2872 0266.

St. Paul's Convent School, 6/F, 140 Leighton Road, Causeway Bay, Hong Kong.

Universities

Chinese University of Hong Kong, 67 Chatham Road South. Tel: 2723 7966. Correspondence Courses. Tel: 2366 0717.

Hong Kong University of Science and Technology, Clearwater Bay. Tel: 2358 888 / 2358 6622.

Hong Kong Polytechnic, Hunghom. Tel: 2766 5111.

LANGUAGE SCHOOLS

Hong Kong English Club, 41 Carnarvon Road. Tel: 2721 2511.

Hong Kong Students English Club, Witty Commercial Building. Tel: 2384 3761.

Kai Tik English Tutorial, Yam Yuck Building. Tel: 2778 2123.

Le Française Moderne, Rm 501, 30-32 D'Aguilar Street, Central. Tel: 2877 6160.

Alliance Française, 123 Hennessey Road. Tel: 2527 7825.

Goethe Institut (German), Hong Kong Arts Centre. Tel: 2802 0088.

Berlitz Language Centre, One Pacific Place. Tel: 2826 9223.

International Putonghua Language Centre, Prospect Building. Tel: 2780 9116.

British Institute, Yue Shung Commercial Building. Tel: 2523 8455.

Mach Mandarin, 22/F Hang Leung Centre, 2 Paterson Street, Causeway Bay. Tel: 2890 7861.

Cambridge Language Institute, 545 Nathan Road, Tsimshatsui, Kowloon. Tel: 2770 3891.

LIBRARIES

Urban Council Public Libraries, 6/F City Hall. Tel: 2921 2669.

American Library, United Centre, 95 Queensway, Admiralty. Tel: 2529 9661.

PROPERTY AGENTS

Knight, Frank and Kan, Bank of China Tower. Tel: 2810 8123.

Chesterton Petty, 28/F 1 Connaught Place, Jardine House. Tel: 2840 1177.

Definite Property, 29B Bonham Road. Tel: 2547 1232.

Hong Kong Real Estate Agencies Association. Tel: 2893 1116.

Hong Kong Real Estate Services Centre. Tel: 2568 1315.

PUBS, CLUBS AND RESTAURANTS

Mad Dogs Pub, 1 D'Aguilar Street, Central. Tel: 2810 1000.

Mad Dogs, 32 Nathan Road, Kowloon. Tel: 2301 2222.

Ned Kelly's Last Stand, 11A Ashley Road, Kowloon. Tel: 2376 0562.

Rick's Cafe, 4 Hart Avenue, Kowloon. Tel: 2367 2939.

Jazz Club, 2/F 34-36 D'Aguilar Street, Central. Tel: 2845 8477.

Bull & Bear, Hutchison House, Central. Tel: 2525 7436.

American Restaurant (Pekingnese), 20 Lockhart Road, Wanchai. Tel: 2527 7277.

Yung Kee Restaurant (Cantonese), 32-40 Wellington Street, Central. Tel: 2522 1624.

Spring Moon (Cantonese), 1/F The Peninsula Hotel, Salisbury Road, Tsimshatsui. Tel: 2739 2322.

Ashoka Restaurant (Indian), G/F Connaught Commercial Building, 185 Wanchai Road, Wanchai. Tel: 2891 8981.

Baan Thai Restaurant (Thai), 4/F Causeway Bay Plaza 1, 489 Hennessey Road, Causeway Bay. Tel: 2831 9155.

Jimmy's Kitchen (Western), LG/F South China Building, 1-3 Wyndham Street, Central. Tel: 2526 5293.

Stanley's French Restaurant (French), 86-88 Stanley Main Street, Stanley. Tel: 2813 8873.

SHIPPING COMPANIES

Allied Pickfords Shipping, Suite 1406, Silvercord Tower 1, 30 Canton Road, Tsimshatsui. Tel: 2736 6032.

Universal Removal, RM 20A, 5-11 Thomson Road, Wanchai. Tel: 2866 0151.

Columbia International Removers, Rm 2213 Hong Kong Plaza, 188 Connaught Road West, Hong Kong. Tel: 2547 6228.

Express Transportation, 4/F 54 Tung Lo Wan Road, Hong Kong. Tel: 2576 6002.

Baltrans International Moving, Unit 1106 Tower 1, 9 Sheung Yuet Road, Kowloon Bay. Tel: 2756 2882.

SPORTS AND SOCIAL CLUBS

Hong Kong Football Club, Sports Road, Happy Valley. Tel: 2882 7470.

Hong Kong Cricket Club, 137 Wongnaichung Gap Road. Tel: 2574 6266.

Hong Kong Rugby Football Union, Development Office 1, Stadium Path, Hong Kong. Tel: 2504 8300.

Clearwater Bay Golf & Country Club, Po Toi O. Tel: 2719 2454.

Underwater Association, Rm 910 Queen Elizabeth Stadium, 18 Oi Kwan Road, Wanchai. Tel: 2572 3792.

Royal Hong Kong Yacht Club, Kellet Island, Causeway Bay. Tel: 2832 2817.

Hong Kong Parachute Club, 126 Kennedy Road. Tel: 2891 5447.

Hong Kong Expatriates Association, Star House. Tel: 2730 9851.

South China Athletics Association, 88 Caroline Hill Road, Causeway Bay. Tel: 2577 6932.

TRANSPORT

China Motor Bus Company, 391 Chaiwan Road. Tel: 2515 1331. Hotline: 2565 8556.

Kowloon Motor Bus Company, 1 Po Lun Street. Tel: 2745 4466.

Hong Kong Tramways, Whitty Street. Tel: 2559 8918 / 2548 7102.

Star Ferry
Edinburgh Place Terminal. Tel: 2522 1236.
East Wanchai Pier. Tel: 2827 6311.
Kowloon Terminal. Tel: 2366 2576.
Hunghom Terminal. Tel: 2333 8409.
Hong Kong & Yaumati Ferry Co. Tel: 2736 1681.
HK China Hydrofoil. Tel: 2736 1629.
HK Hi Speed Ferries (Macau service). Tel: 2815 2789.
HK Macau Hydrofoil Co. Tel: 2521 8302.

MTR Headquarters. Tel: 2758 6625. Hotline: 2750 0170.

TRAVEL

China International Travel Service, 6/F Tower 11, 75 Mody Road,
Tsimshatsui. Tel: 2732 5888.
China Tours, 3/F Cameron Centre, 57-59 Chatham Road, Tsimshatsui. Tel:
2638 3200.
China Travel Service, (Foreign Passenger Dept), 27 Nathan Road,
Tsimshatsui. Tel: 2721 1331.
Travel Industry Council of Hong Kong, Rm 1706-1709 Fortress Tower, 250
Kings Road, North Point. Tel: 2807 1199.
Four Seasons Travel. Tel: 2380 2638.
Concorde Travel. Tel: 2526 3391.
Gateway Travel. Tel: 2722 4388.
Wing On Travel. Tel: 2332 8130.
Tourism Authority of Thailand. Tel: 2868 0732.
Malaysian Tourism Board. Tel: 2528 5810.

Further Reading

GENERAL

Hong Kong: Portraits of Power, Evelyn Huang (Weidenfeld & Nicolson, 1995).

The Fall of Hong Kong: China's Triumph and Britain's Betrayal, Mark Roberti (Wiley, 1994).

Half-Crown Colony: A Hong Kong Notebook, James Pope-Hennessey (Cape, 1969).

Hong Kong: Borrowed Place, Borrowed Time, Richard Hughes (Deutsch, 1968).

City on the Rocks: Hong Kong's Uncertain Future, Kevin Rafferty (Penguin, 1991).

Mouldering Pearl, Hong Kong at the Crossroads, Felix Patrikeeff (Coronet, 1990).

Hong Kong Hong Kong, Dick Wilson (Unwin Hyman, 1990).

Hong Kong: Epilogue to an Empire, Jan Morris (Penguin, 1989).

The Fate of Hong Kong, Gerald Segal (Simon & Schuster, 1993).

In the Mouth of the Dragon: Hong Kong Past, Present and Future, Philip Geddes (Century, 1982).

The Business Environment in Hong Kong, David Lethbridge (Oxford University Press, 1980).

Living and Working in China, Christine Hall (How To Books, 1996).

HISTORY

A History of Hong Kong, Frank Welsh (Harper Collins, 1993).

At the Going Down of the Sun: Hong Kong and South-East Asia 1841-1945, Oliver Lindsay (Hamilton, 1981).

The Lasting Honour: The Fall of Hong Kong, 1941, Oliver Lindsay (Hamilton, 1978).

The Private Life of Old Hong Kong: Western Women in the British Colony, Susanna Hoe (Oxford University Press).

TRAVEL GUIDES

Hong Kong and Macau: The Rough Guide, Jules Brown (Rough Guide, 1993).
Hong Kong, Macau and Taiwan, Nina Nelson (Batsford, 1984).
Hong Kong, Macau & Canton, Robert Storey (Lonely Planet, 1994).
Hong Kong, Collins Traveller, Neil Wilson (Collins, 1990).

NOVELS

Message from Hong Kong, Mignon G Eberhart (Collins, 1969).
The Nine Dragons: A Novel of Hong Kong 1997, Justin Scott (Grafton, 1991).
The Hong Kong Edge, Justin Scott (Grafton, 1990).
Tai Pan: A Novel of Hong Kong, James Clavell (Hodder & Stoughton, 1982).
Hong Kong Honeymoon, Lee Wilkinson (Mills & Boon, 1991).
The Hong Kong Triangle, Mona Newman (Hale, 1981).
Heaven in Hong Kong, Barbara Cartland (Severn House, 1990).

ANNUAL DIGESTS

Hong Kong Annual Digest of Statistics, Census and Statistics Department.
Hong Kong Property Review, Rating and Valuation Department.
Living in Hong Kong, American Chamber of Commerce.
Royal Hong Kong Police Force Review.

HANDBOOKS FOR EXPATS

Working Abroad: Essential Financial Planning for Expatriates and their Employers (How To Books, 1993).
Working on Contract Worldwide: How to Triple Your Earnings by Working as an Independent Contractor Anywhere in the World (How To Books, 1996).
How to Emigrate, Roger Jones (How To Books, 1994).
How to Master Languages, Roger Jones (How To Books, 1993).
Finding Work Overseas: How and where to contact international recruitment agencies, consultancies and employers, Matthew Cunningham (How To Books, 1996).
Obtaining Visas & Work Permits: How and where to obtain the services of immigration lawyers and consultants worldwide, Roger Jones (How To Books, 1996).

Index

How To Books

How To Books provide practical help on a large range of topics. They are available through all good bookshops or can be ordered direct from the distributors. Just tick the titles you want and complete the form on the following page.

___ Apply to an Industrial Tribunal (£7.99)
___ Applying for a Job (£7.99)
___ Applying for a United States Visa (£15.99)
___ Be a Freelance Journalist (£8.99)
___ Be a Freelance Secretary (£8.99)
___ Be a Local Councillor (£8.99)
___ Be an Effective School Governor (£9.99)
___ Become a Freelance Sales Agent (£9.99)
___ Become an Au Pair (£8.99)
___ Buy & Run a Shop (£8.99)
___ Buy & Run a Small Hotel (£8.99)
___ Cash from your Computer (£9.99)
___ Career Planning for Women (£8.99)
___ Choosing a Nursing Home (£8.99)
___ Claim State Benefits (£9.99)
___ Communicate at Work (£7.99)
___ Conduct Staff Appraisals (£7.99)
___ Conducting Effective Interviews (£8.99)
___ Copyright & Law for Writers (£8.99)
___ Counsel People at Work (£7.99)
___ Creating a Twist in the Tale (£8.99)
___ Creative Writing (£9.99)
___ Critical Thinking for Students (£8.99)
___ Do Voluntary Work Abroad (£8.99)
___ Do Your Own Advertising (£8.99)
___ Do Your Own PR (£8.99)
___ Doing Business Abroad (£9.99)
___ Emigrate (£9.99)
___ Employ & Manage Staff (£8.99)
___ Find Temporary Work Abroad (£8.99)
___ Finding a Job in Canada (£9.99)
___ Finding a Job in Computers (£8.99)
___ Finding a Job in New Zealand (£9.99)
___ Finding a Job with a Future (£8.99)
___ Finding Work Overseas (£9.99)
___ Freelance DJ-ing (£8.99)
___ Get a Job Abroad (£10.99)
___ Get a Job in America (£9.99)
___ Get a Job in Australia (£9.99)
___ Get a Job in Europe (£9.99)
___ Get a Job in France (£9.99)
___ Get a Job in Germany (£9.99)
___ Get a Job in Hotels and Catering (£8.99)
___ Get a Job in Travel & Tourism (£8.99)
___ Get into Films & TV (£8.99)
___ Get into Radio (£8.99)
___ Get That Job (£6.99)
___ Getting your First Job (£8.99)
___ Going to University (£8.99)
___ Helping your Child to Read (£8.99)
___ Investing in People (£8.99)
___ Invest in Stocks & Shares (£8.99)

___ Keep Business Accounts (£7.99)
___ Know Your Rights at Work (£8.99)
___ Know Your Rights: Teachers (£6.99)
___ Live & Work in America (£9.99)
___ Live & Work in Australia (£12.99)
___ Live & Work in Germany (£9.99)
___ Live & Work in Greece (£9.99)
___ Live & Work in Italy (£8.99)
___ Live & Work in New Zealand (£9.99)
___ Live & Work in Portugal (£9.99)
___ Live & Work in Spain (£7.99)
___ Live & Work in the Gulf (£9.99)
___ Living & Working in Britain (£8.99)
___ Living & Working in China (£9.99)
___ Living & Working in Hong Kong (£10.99)
___ Living & Working in Israel (£10.99)
___ Living & Working in Japan (£8.99)
___ Living & Working in Saudi Arabia (£12.99)
___ Living & Working in the Netherlands (£9.99)
___ Lose Weight & Keep Fit (£6.99)
___ Make a Wedding Speech (£7.99)
___ Making a Complaint (£8.99)
___ Manage a Sales Team (£8.99)
___ Manage an Office (£8.99)
___ Manage Computers at Work (£8.99)
___ Manage People at Work (£8.99)
___ Manage Your Career (£8.99)
___ Managing Budgets & Cash Flows (£9.99)
___ Managing Meetings (£8.99)
___ Managing Your Personal Finances (£8.99)
___ Market Yourself (£8.99)
___ Master Book-Keeping (£8.99)
___ Mastering Business English (£8.99)
___ Master GCSE Accounts (£8.99)
___ Master Languages (£8.99)
___ Master Public Speaking (£8.99)
___ Obtaining Visas & Work Permits (£9.99)
___ Organising Effective Training (£9.99)
___ Pass Exams Without Anxiety (£7.99)
___ Pass That Interview (£6.99)
___ Plan a Wedding (£7.99)
___ Prepare a Business Plan (£8.99)
___ Publish a Book (£9.99)
___ Publish a Newsletter (£9.99)
___ Raise Funds & Sponsorship (£7.99)
___ Rent & Buy Property in France (£9.99)
___ Rent & Buy Property in Italy (£9.99)
___ Retire Abroad (£8.99)
___ Return to Work (£7.99)
___ Run a Local Campaign (£6.99)
___ Run a Voluntary Group (£8.99)
___ Sell Your Business (£9.99)

___ Selling into Japan (£14.99)	___ Use the Internet (£9.99)
___ Setting up Home in Florida (£9.99)	___ Winning Consumer Competitions (£8.99)
___ Spend a Year Abroad (£8.99)	___ Winning Presentations (£8.99)
___ Start a Business from Home (£7.99)	___ Work from Home (£8.99)
___ Start a New Career (£6.99)	___ Work in an Office (£7.99)
___ Starting to Manage (£8.99)	___ Work in Retail (£8.99)
___ Starting to Write (£8.99)	___ Work with Dogs (£8.99)
___ Start Word Processing (£8.99)	___ Working Abroad (£14.99)
___ Start Your Own Business (£8.99)	___ Working as a Holiday Rep (£9.99)
___ Study Abroad (£8.99)	___ Working in Japan (£10.99)
___ Study & Learn (£7.99)	___ Working in Photography (£8.99)
___ Study & Live in Britain (£7.99)	___ Working in the Gulf (£10.99)
___ Studying at University (£8.99)	___ Working on Contract Worldwide (£9.99)
___ Studying for a Degree (£8.99)	___ Working on Cruise Ships (£9.99)
___ Successful Grandparenting (£8.99)	___ Write a CV that Works (£7.99)
___ Successful Mail Order Marketing (£9.99)	___ Write a Press Release (£9.99)
___ Successful Single Parenting (£8.99)	___ Write a Report (£8.99)
___ Survive at College (£4.99)	___ Write an Assignment (£8.99)
___ Survive Divorce (£8.99)	___ Write an Essay (£7.99)
___ Surviving Redundancy (£8.99)	___ Write & Sell Computer Software (£9.99)
___ Take Care of Your Heart (£5.99)	___ Write Business Letters (£8.99)
___ Taking in Students (£8.99)	___ Write for Publication (£8.99)
___ Taking on Staff (£8.99)	___ Write for Television (£8.99)
___ Taking Your A-Levels (£8.99)	___ Write Your Dissertation (£8.99)
___ Teach Abroad (£8.99)	___ Writing a Non Fiction Book (£8.99)
___ Teach Adults (£8.99)	___ Writing & Selling a Novel (£8.99)
___ Teaching Someone to Drive (£8.99)	___ Writing & Selling Short Stories (£8.99)
___ Travel Round the World (£8.99)	___ Writing Reviews (£8.99)
___ Use a Library (£6.99)	___ Your Own Business in Europe (£12.99)

To: Plymbridge Distributors Ltd, Plymbridge House, Estover Road, Plymouth PL6 7PZ. Customer Services Tel: (01752) 202301. Fax: (01752) 202331.

Please send me copies of the titles I have indicated. Please add postage & packing (UK £1, Europe including Eire, £2, World £3 airmail).

☐ I enclose cheque/PO payable to Plymbridge Distributors Ltd for £ _____

☐ Please charge to my ☐ MasterCard, ☐ Visa, ☐ AMEX card.

Account No. ☐☐☐☐☐☐☐☐☐☐☐☐☐☐☐☐

Card Expiry Date ☐☐ 19 ☎ **Credit Card orders may be faxed or phoned.**

Customer Name (CAPITALS) ....

Address ....

.... Postcode...............

Telephone........................ Signature ....

Every effort will be made to despatch your copy as soon as possible but to avoid possible disappointment please allow up to 21 days for despatch time (42 days if overseas). Prices and availability are subject to change without notice.

Code BPA